13

THE LITTLE BOOK OF

Quick Fixes
FOR THE Home
Handywoman

BRIDGET BODOANO

Quadrille

Editorial Director Jane O'Shea
Art Director Helen Lewis
Designer Chalkley Calderwood Pratt
Project Editor Hilary Mandleberg
Illustrations Bridget Bodoano
Production Bridget Fish

This edition first published in 2006 by
Quadrille Publishing Limited, Alhambra House
27–31 Charing Cross Road, London WC2H 0LS

British Library Cataloguing-in-Publication Data
A catalogue record for this book is available from the British Library.

ISBN-10   1 84400 282 9
ISBN-13   978 184400 282 5

Printed in Singapore

CONTENTS

Introduction

The traditional division of labour with men putting up shelves and grateful women clearing up the mess now seems quaint as well as politically incorrect.

Nowadays it is not unusual for women to be able to cook a meal for four, check the children's homework, download the latest music to our MP3 player and programme the video recorder while also holding down a responsible full-time job, and if that's not enough, many are also tackling the DIY. However, for many of today's busy people their upbringing did not include how to wield a hammer, saw and drill which is why *The Little Book of Tips and Quick Fixes for the Home Handywoman* is so useful (for men too). Packed full of essential tips, useful facts and the quickest of quick fixes, it guides you through the basic home improvement jobs that you're likely to want to tackle. And by learning something of what's hidden behind your walls and beneath your floors, and the sort of problems that can arise when you DIY, you'll be able to judge whether to have a go yourself or leave it to the experts.

This little book offers you common-sense tips ranging from how to choose the essential DIY kit, through learning basic skills and dealing with water and electricity, right through to making simple furniture and assembling a flatpack without resorting to the gin bottle. And if you also missed out on learning the art of housework, there's even advice on how to keep your newly DIYed home spick and span!

So buy yourself a spanking new tool kit and get down to business.

Bridget Bodoano

THE KIT

Handywoman helpline

Q: I'm a total novice when it comes to DIY but I'd like to get started. The problem is, I'm completely stumped when it comes to deciding how much to spend on my tools. There's such a wide range of prices. Can you help?

A: For items such as basic hand tools, the price will reflect the quality. For a beginner though, the cheaper tools are usually perfectly adequate. For anything that involves machinery, motors or electricity it's usually better to go for a reputable, well-known brand. Then you can be sure that what you buy will conform to the necessary standards and safety regulations.

Ten tool tips

1 Treat yourself to a smart box or bag with compartments or pockets to store your tools.

2 Make sure your toolkit is easily accessible.

3 Always put tools back in their box or bag once you have finished with them.

4 Keep any instructions for use with the tools.

5 Buy a power drill that comes in a handy bag with storage for all its kit.

Keep all sharp blades covered when not in use.

 Carefully throw away all old disposable blades.

 Always keep a pair of rubber gloves, goggles, a mask and some plasters in your toolkit.

 Keep screwdriver sets and spanners together in their original packaging or in a natty pocketed roll.

 For a safe and comfortable grip, always choose power tools that fit your handsize and are not too heavy.

Do your homework

The range of tools on offer in most DIY stores is large, but information is scarce, so do a little research before you shop. Browsing through catalogues and looking on internet is a good way to discover the function and power of different products. Many companies have a helpline where assistants dispense the right sort of advice (and don't mind in the least if you don't know your chuck from your elbow).

What do I need?

There's a huge number of frightening-looking and fancy tools on the market, but most basic DIY jobs can be done with a select few.

BRADAWL: A short, sharp spike on a chunky handle. Used for marking the position of and making pilot holes (see page 33).

CUTTING KNIFE: With a chunky, easy-to-grip handle with a strong replaceable blade, a cutting knife is used for cutting everything from cardboard to carpet.

SPIRIT LEVEL: A device that shows whether surfaces and edges are truly horizontal or vertical. Vital for putting up shelves.

CLAW HAMMER: Essential for knocking in nails, but more frequently for taking them out. Also invaluable for minor demolition work.

TAPE MEASURE: For measuring rooms or marking out smaller distances. A medium-width 3m (10ft) tape measure will fit nicely in your hand.

TRY SQUARE: Useful for marking lengths of wood and cutting and checking right angles.

SCREWDRIVERS: A slotted-head screwdriver has a flat point and is used for screws with a straight slot in the head. A cross-head screwdriver is used for screws with a cross-shaped slot. You'll need both in various sizes and lengths. Power screwdrivers are easier, faster and screw tighter – and in reverse gear they're great for undoing screws.

SPANNERS: For tightening and undoing nuts and bolts. Adjustable spanners can be altered to fit any size bolt but are a bit fiddly.

PLIERS: For gripping objects so you can turn, squeeze, pinch or pull out a variety of things, from nails in awkward corners to screw tops that won't unscrew. They often have a facility for wire-cutting too. Blunt-nose pliers are good for general use but the long-nose variety are useful for fiddly work.

SAWS: Buy an all-purpose saw for cutting wood, metal and plastics. Also invest in a small hacksaw with a thin, replaceable blade, which is useful for cutting metal and plastic pipes.

Resist temptation

There are several tempting-looking power tools on the market but to start with, resist buying anything other than a power drill. Power planers, circular saws and belt sanders need a higher level of skill and can always be hired if necessary.

All power to your elbow

Motor power is expressed in watts: the higher the wattage the more powerful and versatile the tool. Power drills, for example, usually range from 500W to 1000W.

Five things to look for when buying a power drill

1 POWER: You'll need 700W to 800W if you want to drill into masonry.

2 VARIABLE SPEED: Speed is given in revs per minute (rpm). Most general-purpose drills go up to 3000 rpm. You need a lower speed for drilling into particularly hard surfaces, and a faster speed for wood, to give a neat finish and prevent splitting. A slow speed is also necessary if you want to use the drill as a screwdriver.

3 REVERSE: Reverse is essential if you're going to use the drill to remove as well as drive in screws. It also comes in handy if the drill bit gets stuck.

HAMMER OR PERCUSSION ACTION:
This is necessary for drilling
in masonry.

ATTACHMENTS: Often a range of
accessories can be added for sanding
and polishing. You never know when
they may come in handy.

Corded versus cordless

Cordless tools were developed for use in places where being attached to a power cable can be difficult or dangerous, such as outside or up a tall ladder. While cable-free drilling is undoubtedly convenient, there are disadvantages. For example, the power isn't consistent – it will lessen as the battery runs down – and it can be a bit of a drag remembering to re-charge the battery. Buy a spare and keep it on charge so it's ready for use when the first battery goes flat.

If you're using a corded tool it can be just as convenient but always be aware of the cable. Don't get entangled in it and, if it's too short to allow free movement, use an extension lead.

'Buy a spare and keep it on charge so it's ready for use when the first battery goes flat.'

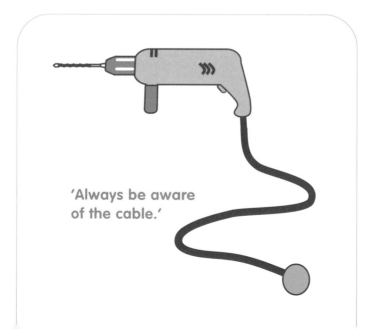

'Always be aware of the cable.'

MAKING A
HOLE

A bit about bits

The part of the drill that actually makes the hole is called the bit. Bits come in a variety of shapes and sizes suited to different functions and materials. They're sized in millimetres. The most widely used range from 2mm to 10mm.

✳ **A MASONRY BIT** has a tungsten-carbide tip and is used for plaster, concrete and brick.

✳ **A WOOD BIT** has a sharp cutting thread and a point for accurate positioning.

✳ **A METAL BIT** is made from hard steel and has a v-shaped tip. As well as being used for cutting metal, it can also be used for wood.

✳ **A COUNTERSINK BIT** has a short, wide pointed end. It drills a shallow cone-shaped recess in wood for countersinking screws – so that when the screw is in place, its head is flush with, or below the surface of the wood. The recess can then be filled with wood filler to give a smooth surface.

✳ **A FLAT WOOD BIT** has a central point and flat steel either side. It is used to drill a fairly large hole in wood.

Drilling drill

Before drilling into any wall, floor or ceiling
you must check in case there's an electricity
cable, gas or water pipe so you can avoid
making a hole in it. So don't drill near power
sockets or immediately above, below or
around light switches or light fittings.

You can buy inexpensive, battery-powered
devices that light up to indicate the presence
of metal pipework in walls or under floors,
or to detect the position of electrical cables.

How deep, how wide?

The depth and diameter of the hole you need to drill will depend on the size of the screw and, if you are using one, the length of the wallplug (see page 67). To ensure the hole is the right length, wrap a piece of tape around the drill bit to mark the depth required or use an adjustable depth stop – sometimes supplied with a power drill.

Remember that a certain amount of dust and debris will collect at the far end of the hole as you drill, so you need to drill a little deeper than the length of the wallplug.

Handywoman helpline

Q: It's sometimes difficult to get a screw into a piece of wood. Can you suggest any tips?

A: A screw will go into wood more easily and more accurately if there's a pilot hole to start if off. You can make one using a bradawl or a drill with a fine bit. Similarly, if you are putting up hooks or fixings with a screw thread, they'll also be easier to screw in with a pilot hole.

Nails don't normally need a drilled hole but if they're very long or the wood is very thick, they'll also benefit from a pilot hole. This will reduce the risk of the nail bending, going in at the wrong angle or splitting the wood.

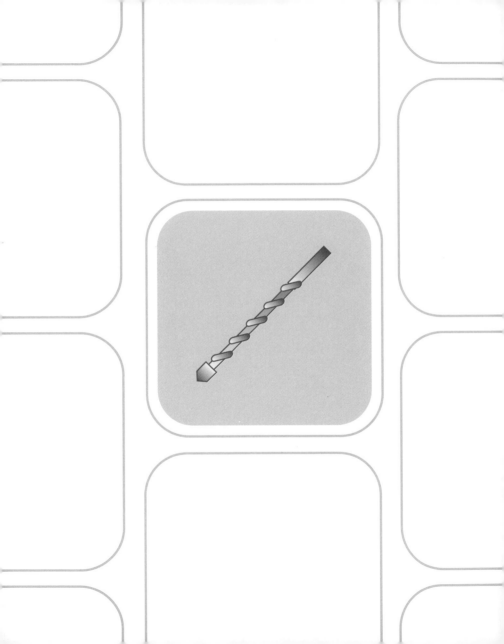

The drill for special surfaces

✳ To avoid cracking or chipping ceramic tiles when you drill them, stick a piece of masking tape on top of the tile to help locate the drill bit and stop it slithering and shooting off across the tile. Use a masonry bit but set the drill to rotary action and use a slow speed.

✳ When drilling into fairly soft metal, make a small dent with a nail punch or a bradawl and place the v-shaped end of the metal bit into this dent before starting to drill.

✳ Always drill downwards through the top of plastic-coated laminate. Drilling upwards from below can crack it.

Drilling a hole in a wall

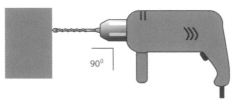

1 Check there are no wires or pipes in the wall. Mark the centre of the hole. Place the point of the drill bit firmly on this mark at a 90-degree angle to the wall.

2 Turn on the drill. Keeping it as level and straight as possible, push the drill bit gently into the wall. Continue pushing until the hole is drilled to the depth required.

3 Insert a wallplug (see page 67) into the drilled hole and tap gently into place with a hammer.

4 To fix your item (such as a coat hook), place it against the wall so the screw hole and drilled hole line up, insert the screw, hold firmly in place and tighten with a screwdriver.

Drilling a hole for a pipe

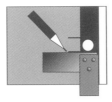

1 Mark the cutting lines on each side of the pipe.

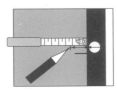

2 Measure the distance from the wall to the front of the pipe and mark this distance on the shelf/worktop.

3 Mark the centre of the hole to be drilled. This is where you position the drill bit.

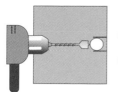

4 Drill out the hole using a power drill fitted with a flat wood bit.

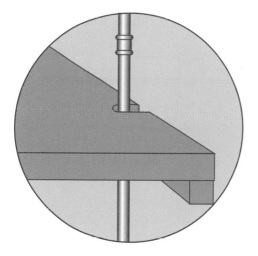

5 Cut along the marked lines using a saw, then fit the cut surface around the pipe.

CUTTING

Get a grip

It helps to have a simple workbench with clamps or a vice to hold the piece you're cutting between two lengths of wood. The workbench also gives you a level surface to work on and the clamps can also be used to hold things you're drilling or sanding.

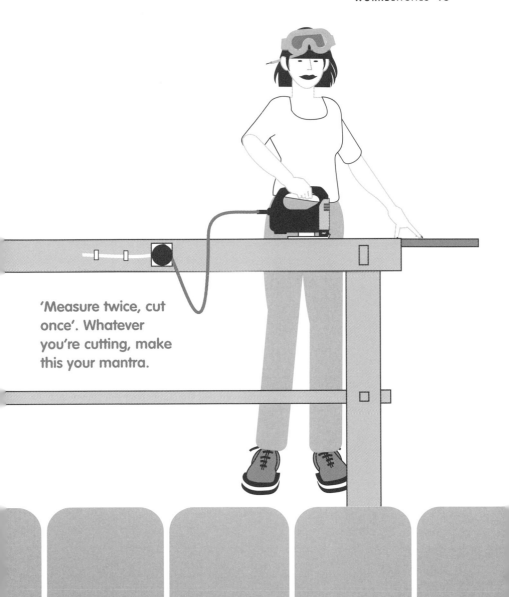

'Measure twice, cut once'. Whatever you're cutting, make this your mantra.

Handywoman helpline

Q: I can never seem to manage to use a handsaw properly. Are there any special pointers I should bear in mind?

A: Start by placing the blade of the saw on the marked spot on the edge of the wood. Then dig the blade gently into the wood and draw it backwards a little way to cut a small nick. Using the nick to locate the saw blade – and making sure that it's vertical and is lined up with the cutting line – start sawing by pushing the blade forwards and pulling it backwards, always cutting down at an angle of 90 degrees.

HANDYWOMAN SAWING TIP

To begin with you may find the saw sticks and you have to keep re-starting, but once you get into a regular rhythm, try not to stop until you have cut through.

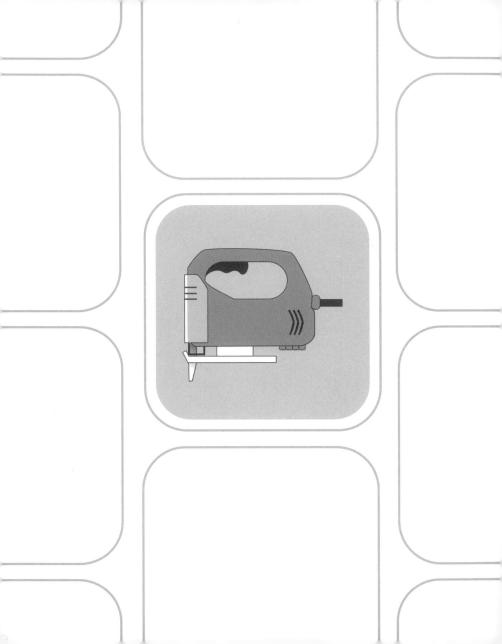

Power jigsaws

A power jigsaw isn't that difficult to use and
will give a neater, straighter cut than a
handsaw, and with a lot less effort. Most will
make straight and curved cuts in wood up
to about 70mm (2¾ inches) thick and in metal
up to 5mm (¼ inch) thick, as well as in most
plastics. Variable speed allows you to slow
down for tricky bits and a dustblower keeps
the cutting line visible – some models even
extract the dust as you go.

A professional cut

For large pieces of timber and long cuts, it sometimes pays to have a professional job. Most DIY stores will cut wood (straight cuts only) to your exact measurements. The service is often free or carries only a small charge.

Before you go shopping, check the dimensions of standard lengths and widths of timber so you can work out the most economical way of buying what you need. Draw diagrams of your requirements and mark on the measurements.

Once you have bought the timber you need, load it into your trolley and take it, along with your diagrams, to the cutting-service area. Sometimes these services are much in demand and queues build up so if at all possible, don't ask for too much to be cut at one time. Or try to go at less busy times.

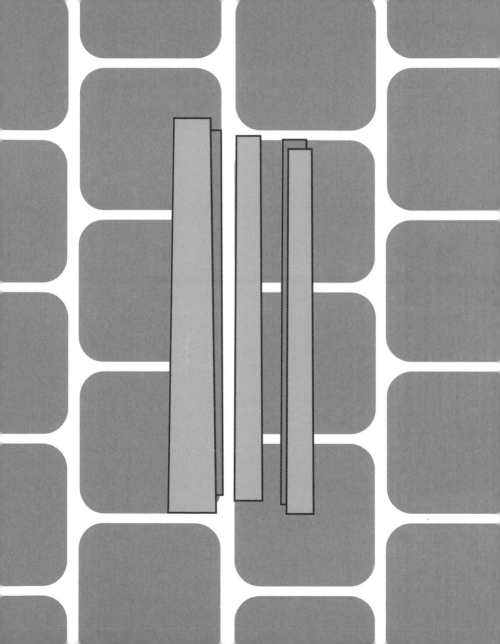

Cutting plastics

Plastic edging and piping are easy enough to cut, but sheeting is more troublesome. Soft plastic can clog the teeth of the saw and thicker, harder materials, such as acrylic sheeting, will crack unless cut carefully. Acrylics are also expensive so it's best to have them cut and finished professionally.

Cutting tiles

A platform or tile cutter (see page 136) will make clean straight cuts in ceramic tiles, but for awkward shapes you'll need to use a pair of tile nibblers (see page 136). These require care and a certain amount of skill.

Cutting cables

Pliers have a cutting blade that cuts electric cables and wiring and some have a notch for stripping the plastic sheathing off wires.

Light cuts...

Cutting knives can be used for paper, vinyl, carpet and thin plastic. Those with replaceable blades are versatile as you can get a variety of blades such as a small saw blade and a curved blade for cutting carpet.

...and heavy cuts

For cutting through thick metal, ceramic or stone, you'll need to resort to an angle grinder. This power tool has a tough, circular blade that whizzes round really fast. It isn't expensive and looks small and manageable, but the effort needed and the noise and dust it generates during use means it's more suited to builders than beginners.

Metal special

✳ Cutting metal is easier than it sounds but to begin with it's best to avoid cutting sheet metal or heavy metal fittings or fixings.

✳ Metal tubing is frequently used for curtain poles, wardrobe fittings and pipework. To cut it, use a small hacksaw with a thin, replaceable blade. This works adequately, but it can be difficult to control as the blade is quite flexible.

✳ Alternatively, use a pipe cutter. This is an ingenious device that holds the pipe in place while a small blade, tightened by a hand-turned screw, makes a neat, straight cut.

✳ Cutting metal produces a lot of heat, so don't touch the edges of the metal or the saw until things have cooled down.

✳ Tidy up ragged edges with a file or abrasive paper but be careful not to cut your fingers on any sharp metal.

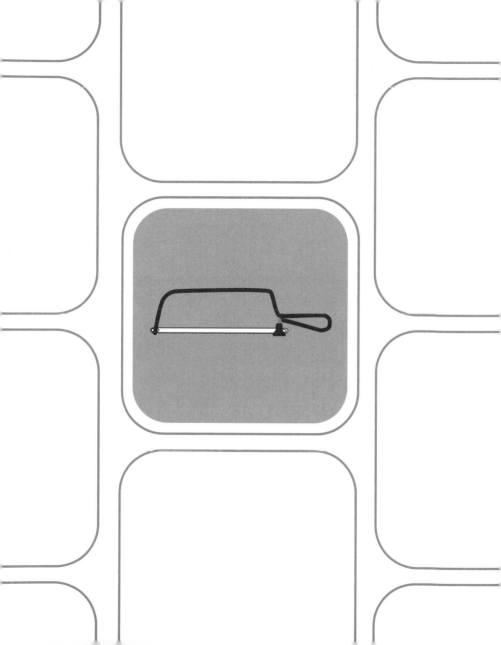

JOINING

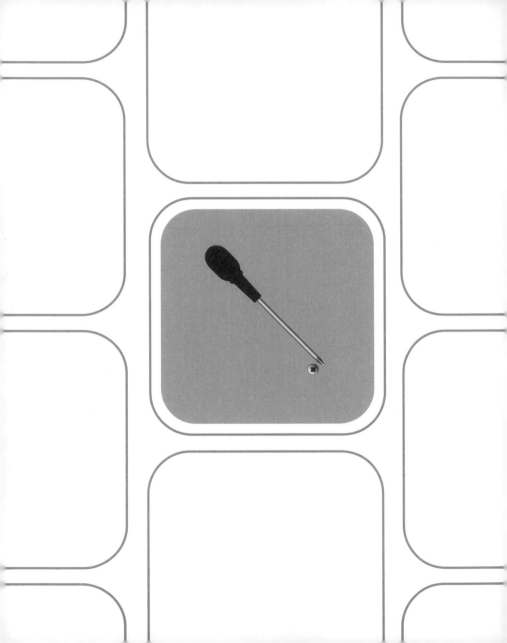

Join up here

Many DIY jobs involve fixing things to walls, fixing things to other things and joining things together. Most things are fixed by means of screws, nails, bolts, glue or, occasionally, double-sided sticky tape. What you use for the job depends on:

FUNCTION: What's the thing I'm fixing supposed to do?

MATERIAL: What's it made of?

SIZE: How big is the thing I'm fixing?

LOAD-BEARING REQUIREMENTS: How much weight does it have to carry or how much stress will it be under?

AESTHETIC CONSIDERATIONS: How will it look?

Why choose nails?

✳ They're easy to use.

✳ They only require a hammer and a steady hand to knock them into place.

Which nail?

WIRE NAIL Unless you're into serious building work you'll mostly use wire nails. The shaft has an oval cross-section and the nail has a solid, slim head.

LOST-HEAD NAILS These have a head that isn't much wider than the shaft of the nail. They're less visible and can be knocked below the surface of the wood with a nail punch.

TACKS These are short, tapered, easy-to-use nails with a large head and a sharp point. They're mostly for fixing carpet and fabric.

PANEL PINS These thin nails with a small head are used when screws would be too big and would split the wood, such as when you are fixing panels or boxing in. They go in easily and are barely visible.

HANDYWOMAN NAILING TIP

Locate a nail by holding it in position and giving it several short taps until it is in far enough to stay put. Then you can drive it in fully with heavier blows without endangering your thumb.

SHORTCUT TO NAILING SUCCESS

For very short nails or tacks where there is no room for fingers, push the nail into a small square of thin card which is easier to hold in position and can be torn away when the nail is firmly located in the wall.

Why choose screws?

✳ They provide a stronger grip and better support.

✳ They're easy to unscrew if you make a mistake, want to take something down or move it to a different position.

✳ They're essential for fixing panelling that may need to be removed for access to plumbing, electricity or gas.

Did you know that...?

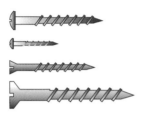

...screws are described by length and diameter. This is referred to as the gauge and ranges from 1 to 20, 20-gauge being the thickest. The most commonly used gauges are 6, 8 and 10. The size depends on use – thicker and longer for heavy jobs to bear a lot of weight, and slimmer ones for thinner materials and lighter jobs.

Easy does it

Screwing into wood is relatively easy.
The thread of the screw digs its own made-
to-measure hole where it sits nice and tight.
Some screws have sharp points and special
threads for screwing directly into the wood
but a pilot hole (see page 33) will make putting
them in much easier and more accurate.

Handywoman helpline

Q: I often can't seem to get the screw to tighten properly. What am I doing wrong?

A: If this happens, the screw may be too short or too thin for the hole, the hole may not be providing a suitable grip, the material you are screwing into may be too soft or too hard, or the wallplug (see page 67) you're using may not be large enough.

Fixing a screw when there's nothing to grip

To get screws to stay in, you must provide something for them to grip on to. This means you are going to have problems screwing into hollow walls, hollow doors, masonry and plasterboard.

✳ Hollow-wall and door fixings, sometimes called 'toggle' fixings, enable a screw to be fixed into a hollow wall or door where a normal screw and plug wouldn't work. You drill a hole, put the fixing into it and screw it tight. As you do so, the outer part of the fixing folds up against the inner face of the wall or panel to keep the screw firmly in place.

✳ For a screw to grip securely into masonry, you must use a wallplug. These are commonly made of plastic and come in sizes to suit all screws. Make your hole with a drill and hammer the wallplug into it (see page 37), then screw the screw in place. Make sure the screw goes into the wallplug and not over to one side.

✳ There are a number of other plugs for use on soft masonry or on plasterboard. Threaded plugs will screw directly into the wall. Nailable plugs consist of a nail with a plug attached which is hammered into a pre-drilled hole.

Simple joints

 The simplest way to join two pieces of wood together is with a butt joint, where two edges are butted together and secured with nails, pins, screws or wood glue. This kind of joint is fine if it's going to be covered up or painted.

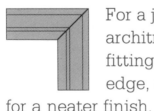 Plain skirting board can be joined using a simple butt joint.

For a job such as putting new architrave around a door or fitting beading around a floor edge, a mitred joint is necessary for a neater finish.

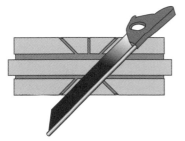

Making a mitred joint involves cutting an accurate 45-degree angle which can be constructed using simple maths and a protractor or, if you are working on narrow strips of wood, a mitre block. A mitre block has 45-degree slots for accurate cuts.

Flatpack fixings

Fixings required to assemble flatpack
furniture are normally included in the pack.
They're made specifically for the product so
may look different from standard fixings.
For tightening bolts you may need an Allen
key. This fits snugly into a hexagonal socket
in the head of a bolt and is then turned.
These are often supplied with the product
but if not, a set of several different sizes can
be bought quite cheaply.

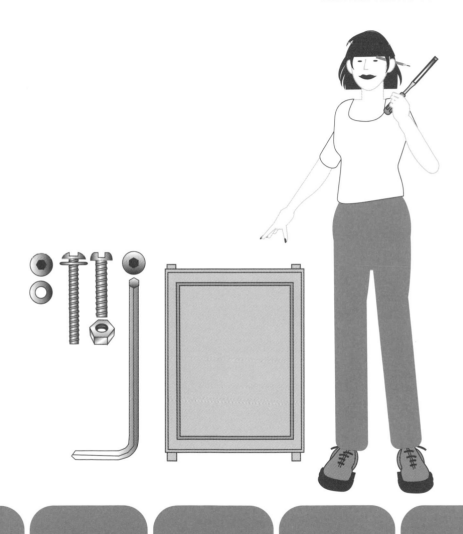

The pros of glue...

✳ Modern adhesives are very efficient.

✳ Some are strong enough to be used instead of nails or screws.

✳ They can be useful for poor-quality or hollow walls that may be unsuitable for screws or nails, or in places or situations such as an awkward corner or proximity to wiring or pipework, where putting in a nail or screw could be difficult or even dangerous.

✳ PVA wood adhesives can be used in addition to nails and screws to strengthen woodworking joints.

...and the cons

✸ Positioning must be accurate.

✸ It isn't easy handling and manoeuvring long lengths of wood coated in quick-drying adhesive.

✸ Anything stuck down will be difficult to remove without damaging the item that is stuck and the surface it is stuck to, whereas nails and screws can be removed relatively easily.

Batten beauties

Putting up a batten – a strip of wood screwed to the wall to which other items can be fixed – is a passport to greater things and once you've done it you'll feel you've earned a certain amount of DIY cred. A batten can be used to support shelving, worktops, cupboards or other heavy weights such as a large picture. It can also be used as a framework for boxing in pipes or putting up wall panelling, and can be useful for attaching things to a hollow wall where the batten can be fixed securely to solid wood studs. Or, if you want, it can simply be used to support a row of coat hooks.

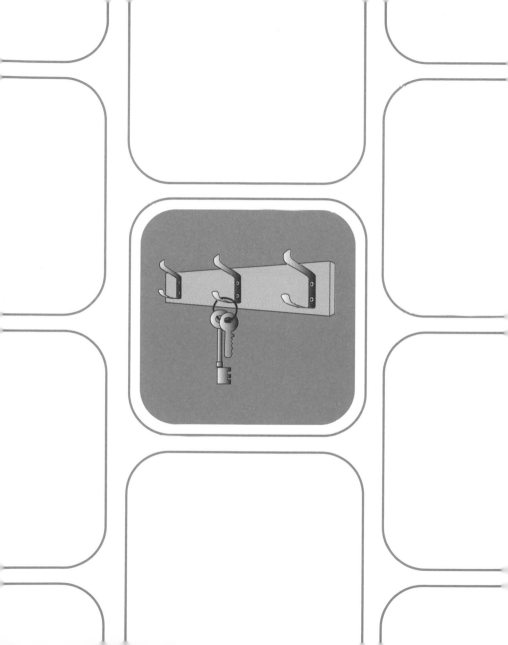

Putting up a batten

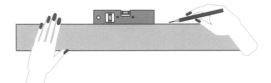

1 Cut the batten to the length required. Hold it in position against the wall using a spirit level to ensure it's perfectly horizontal and draw a pencil line on the wall across the top. Mark the position of the ends. Place the batten on a work surface, mark the position of the screws, making sure they are evenly spaced, then drill through.

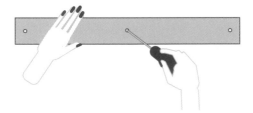

2 Place the batten against the wall and make an indentation in the wall through each of the holes in the batten.

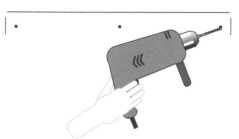

3 Drill holes in the wall at the indentations using a power drill. Pop a wallplug into each drilled hole.

4 Fix the batten to the wall using screws that are long enough to go right through the batten and into the wallplugs.

Six joining projects to do in a weekend

1 Sort out your music collection by putting up a wall-mounted CD rack.

2 Make sure you're never caught out again by installing new bathroom fittings including a loo-roll holder.

3 Make a coat rack by screwing a row of simple hooks to a batten fixed to the wall.

4 Keep your bathroom tidy by fixing up a new medicine cabinet, complete with mirror for those essential make-up checks.

Avoid those last-minute searches for your house or car keys by putting up a hook inside the front door (but make sure it's not in reach of the letter box).

6 Decorate your walls by at last hanging up that heavy picture frame or mirror.

PAINTING

Did you know that...?

...paint can completely change the look and mood of a room. It can make it look cleaner, bigger, cosier, sexier, smarter or just plain nicer. It's also a well-known fact that when selling a property, a coat of paint can turn your house from impossible to incredible.

Handywoman helpline

Q: There's such a huge range of paints on the market, I never know where to start … and that's before I even think about choosing a colour! Can you help?

A. A water-based emulsion is best for internal walls. It's easy to apply and to wash out of brushes, rollers – and your hair. Available in matt or silk finish, emulsion also comes in a huge range of colours. What's more, it's quick-drying and hardly smells.

The dense chalky finish of distemper is historically correct and is particularly suitable for painting the internal walls of old properties. But it's less stable than emulsion and will rub off, so is unsuitable for areas of high wear such as staircases.

When it comes to woodwork, gloss paint is hardwearing but shows up all imperfections and needs careful application. Traditionally, gloss is solvent-based and so is smelly and slow to dry, but water-based versions are now available.

Eggshell, satin and soft-sheen paints are alternatives for woodwork. Some are now water-based. They're much easier to use than gloss and won't show up every imperfection.

Flat paint – usually oil-based – has a dead matt finish. It can also be used on plaster and papered walls.

How much paint?

✳ The amount of paint required for a job will depend on the type and make of paint, the colour, state and porosity of the existing surface and the method of application.

✳ Details of estimated coverage will be printed on the tin – usually in square metres per litre or per can. Five litres of emulsion should cover 60–65 square metres (645–700 square feet).

✳ Extra coats will be necessary to cover a dark colour or pattern. Pure, deep colours, such as bright yellows or reds, will need extra coats too.

All about brushes

❋ For painting walls, invest in a good-quality flat, 150-mm (6-inch) wide brush.

❋ For window frames and architraves you'll need a range of narrower brushes and for larger areas of woodwork, such as doors, you should have a slightly wider brush.

❋ Narrow cutting-in brushes have the bristles cut at an angle to make it easier to get right to the edge when painting glazing bars.

❋ The very cheapest brushes – often sold in bargain sets – will shed their bristles and won't hold the paint well, so are best avoided.

❋ The most expensive brushes have high-quality, densely packed real bristles for ease of application and a smooth finish.

✳ Unless you're planning a lot of decorating (and are prepared to take great care of your brushes) go for a medium price range.

HANDYWOMAN BRUSH BUYING TIP
Check that the bristles spring back when you bend them.

HANDYWOMAN NEW BRUSH TIP
All brushes shed a few bristles when they're new so before using them on woodwork (where shedding bristles will spoil the finish) break them in by using with emulsion first.

What a mess!

Painting is a messy business so make sure you have enough dust sheets to protect furniture, floors and other surfaces from paint splashes and from the water and debris that is inevitable when you wash and strip down walls. Old sheets and bedspreads make perfect dust sheets but use plastic sheeting underneath on vulnerable surfaces as big blobs of paint can soak through fabric.

Handywoman helpline

Q: Why do I always end up with the paint running down my hand when I'm painting and why do I usually get such a poor finish?

A: First of all, it's important not to overload the brush. Dip only a third of the bristles into the paint and wipe off any excess on the side of the tin before painting. And when you paint, use vertical strokes – not dabs or sploshes – and spread the paint out using horizontal strokes as well. On large areas don't brush out too thinly at the edges as this will contribute to your uneven finish.

Roll me over

* Rollers are fantastic for covering large areas of wall or ceiling quickly and evenly.

* Most roller sleeves are either sheepskin (real or synthetic) or foam.

* Long-pile sheepskin holds a lot of paint but medium-pile is more manageable.

* Foam sleeves are less efficient as they tend to leave air bubbles on the surface.

* Roller and tray sets are often very inexpensive and although the quality may not be tip-top, you can just throw them away after use.

* Long-handled roller extensions are helpful for painting ceilings and floors.

* Use a small roller on a long handle when you have to paint behind a radiator, a special

shaped roller for painting into corners, and a small dense foam roller with gloss or eggshell paint for any large flat areas such as doors and bath panels.

Shortcut to roller success

Before painting walls and ceilings with a roller, do a bit of 'cutting in' – using a small brush to paint round all the ceiling/wall joins, corners, skirting boards, light switches and light fittings. Then you can roller away to your heart's content.

Paint-pad perfection

Paint pads are very useful for painting large flat areas and are generally thought to be as good as a roller. They consist of a layer of short mohair pile attached to a foam layer, which gives flexibility and keeps the pad in contact with uneven surfaces. The pad is fixed to a plastic frame with an integrated handle. Also sold in sets with a tray, the best type of tray has a loading roller to ensure the paint is distributed evenly on the pad.

To use, keep the pad flat against the surface and paint in all directions with a gentle sweeping action.

Eight must-have painting prep tools

Using the right tools makes preparation easier as well as more effective.

 Scrapers are used for removing wallpaper or paint. They have flat, non-flexible blades.

 Spokeshaves are useful for removing paint from awkward corners and mouldings.

 Wallpaper scorers are used to puncture the surface of coated or painted wallpaper.

 Steam strippers are held against the wall so the steam penetrates the paper and makes it easier to remove.

5 Hot-air strippers heat and soften solvent-based paint so it can be scraped off easily.

6 Liquid paint strippers break down the adhesive bond between the wallpaper and the wall.

7 Scrubbing brushes are useful for cleaning dirt from corners.

8 Dry paintbrushes can be used as dusting brushes to clean corners and keyholes.

Get that paper off!

If you need to remove old wallpaper, find a hidden corner and remove a little to get an idea of how many layers there are, what type of paper it is, whether it'll come away easily and the state of the wall beneath. If lots of plaster comes away with the paper, it may be best to leave well alone and paint over the top or get a builder in to re-plaster.

Uncoated paper should come off easily with wallpaper stripper mixed with warm water, or by steaming. Coated wallpapers and paper that has been painted over will need scoring first with a wallpaper scorer or with the edge of a scraper. If the paper is vinyl-coated you can usually remove it by simply lifting the corners of the vinyl and pulling it away from its backing paper. The backing can then be removed with wallpaper stripper.

Wall prep

If the old paint surface has loose flakes of paint, use wet-and-dry paper to smooth their edges. Alternatively, use a nylon pan scourer. If, after filling in any holes and cracks (see page 182), the surface still looks a bit flaky, you can give the wall a coat of PVA bonding diluted in water to seal the surface – just follow the instructions on the tin.

A PVA solution is also good for sealing new or newly revealed bare plaster, or you can use a diluted coat of emulsion for this.

HANDYWOMAN TIPS FOR UNEVEN WALLS

If, despite priming, rubbing down and filling, your wall surface is still uneven, you can either learn to love the 'distressed' effect or paint it with a roller to give a slightly textured finish that will soften the blemishes. Alternatively, cover the wall with a thick, textured lining paper and paint over.

Six steps to perfect woodwork prep

1 Wash down and key old woodwork using warm water and sugar soap or detergent.

2 Get rid of blemishes and provide a key with a nylon pan scourer.

3 Sand down any old drips and wrinkles.

4 Hard gloss paint may need further rubbing down with fine wet-and-dry paper.

Repair chips and damaged areas with primer, building up the surface with several coats if necessary and rubbing down between each.

 Wipe down with a clean cloth dipped in white spirit to get rid of any remaining dust and grease.

HANDYWOMAN WALL AND CEILING STAIN TIP

Cover stains such as damp or mildew with a stain block or recommended primer, but address the source of the stain first to prevent the stains reappearing.

If you cover any damp with an impervious coating, it will only send the moisture elsewhere where it could do more damage.

Bare all

✳ When you use a hot-air paint stripper, make sure to keep it moving or you'll end up with burnt wood.

✳ Use a narrow nozzle on glazing bars, to keep the heat away from the window glass.

✳ When you use chemical paint stripper, follow the instructions, make sure there's plenty of ventilation, and wear a mask and good protective gloves as the stripper burns the skin. Don't use on large areas as the fumes are too overpowering.

✳ If you're stripping paint ready for repainting, a bit of residue is OK if it's rubbed down and free of grease. But if you want the bare-wood look you'll have to work hard to get every bit off. Use chemical paint stripper or a combination of that and a hot-air stripper.

Primers and sealers

Special primers and sealers are used to prepare certain surfaces for painting.

STABILISING PRIMER: A white or clear liquid used on walls to bind dusty, powdery and flaky surfaces.

WOOD PRIMER: Available in solvent-based, water-based, acrylic or aluminium forms. Used on new or bare wood to seal and prevent paint soaking into the wood.

GENERAL-PURPOSE PRIMER: Used for wood, metal and plaster as well as for porous building materials. Look out for water-based versions.

METAL PRIMER: Prevents corrosion and provides a key for paint. Rust inhibitors are also available.

PVA BONDING AGENT: A liquid adhesive which, when diluted, can be used as a primer and sealer before you paint (see page 102).

Undercover story

Undercoat is a matt coating that you need to use on woodwork to cover primer as well as any minor imperfections. It provides a smooth, dense surface for your topcoat and is particularly effective if the topcoat is a dark colour or has a high-gloss finish.

Ten handywoman painting tips

1 Work from right to left if you're right-handed (the other way round if you're left-handed) so that your arm is away from your body.

2 For woodwork, your brushstrokes should be vertical or horizontal (according to the direction of the grain of the wood) to prevent brushmarks spoiling the finished surface.

3 For a neat line along skirting boards, around door- and window frames, and between ceiling and wall, place the brush a short distance away from the edge and press down so the bristles fan out to reach the edge.

Be careful not to disturb soft paint and don't try to neaten up edges until the paint is hard.

For a high-quality finish on your woodwork, apply two or three topcoats and rub down carefully with wire wool or wet-and-dry paper between each coat.

To avoid drips, runs and sags, make sure there isn't too much paint on your brush/roller and brush it out across the surface.

Brush out any runs as you go, but don't attempt to brush them out once the surface has started to dry.

8 To avoid specks and lumps on the surface, make sure your brush is clean and that the surface is completely free of dirt and dust.

9 During a break put the lids back on tins and put brushes, rollers or pads (complete with their trays) inside a sealed plastic bag to stop them drying out and attracting dust and dirt.

10 To avoid a patchy finish on walls, only take a break when an entire wall is complete.

'To avoid drips,
make sure there
isn't too much paint
on your brush.'

Clean up your act

✱ Try to clean brushes and other equipment as soon as you've finished work or the paint will harden and be more difficult to remove. If this isn't possible then put them in a plastic bag or leave them to soak in plenty of water.

✱ For water-based paints, wash brushes, rollers and pads in plenty of warm soapy water and rinse until the water is clear.

✱ For solvent-based paints, wipe off excess paint on newspaper then flex the bristles in a jar of white spirit or paint remover to dissolve the remaining paint. Wash with hot soapy water and rinse. Repeat until the brush is clean.

HANDYWOMAN KEEP-IN-SHAPE TIP
Keep paintbrushes in shape by folding paper around the bristles and securing with a rubber band.

PAPERING

Novice notes

✳ If you're a complete wallpapering novice, think very carefully before embarking on wallpapering a room. If the room is large, has high ceilings, is very irregular in shape, or has more than one window and door, it's better to call in a professional or stick to paint.

✳ For your first attempt, why not paper just one wall or a chimney breast? That way you avoid corners, overlaps and having to cut round light switches.

✳ Alternatively, start with a very small room with no awkward features and stick to wallpaper patterns that won't look obvious if they don't quite line up. Avoid ceilings if possible.

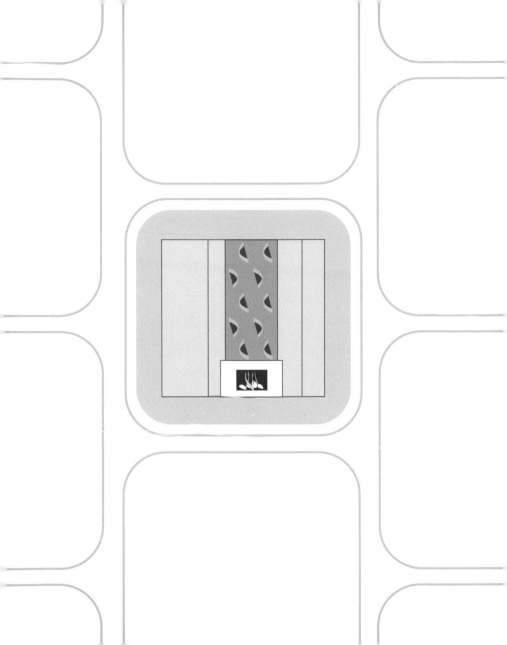

Spoiled for choice

LINING PAPER Plain, buff-coloured paper used over slightly uneven or impervious surfaces to create a suitable paint surface. Also used underneath heavy or expensive wallcoverings.

WOODCHIP PAPER Made by sandwiching particles of wood between two layers of paper. Inexpensive and easy to hang, it covers poor plaster and uneven surfaces. Must be painted.

TEXTURED PAPER Heavily embossed with a variety of patterns, from traditional designs to more modern, abstract ones. Rarely used on every wall; more often used below a dado rail or on a ceiling. Always painted.

PRINTED PAPER An enormous range of designs and colours from small spriggy flowers to bold geometrics and famous designs from the past. The thickness and quality varies and will be reflected in the price.

READY-PASTED PAPER Some wallcoverings are pre-coated with an adhesive that is activated by soaking in cold water.

COATED PAPER A thin coating of PVA is applied to printed papers to create an impervious, washable surface for bathrooms and kitchens. Vinyl wallcoverings consist of a paper or cotton backing with the pattern printed onto a vinyl coating and fused into the surface using heat. Often sold ready-pasted.

WALLPAPER BORDERS Borders of varying designs and widths are often intended for use with a co-ordinating paper but can be used on their own on a painted wall. Some are ready-pasted.

VINTAGE PAPERS A number of shops and market stalls sell rolls of original old wallpaper, especially from the fifties and sixties. It's rare to get any quantity but these can become a fabulous focus of an interior.

Six wallpapering must-haves

1 **PASTING TABLE:** Cheap and very useful. It's the right size – just a little wider than the average roll of paper – and a good working height – slightly higher than a dining table. It's light and can be moved around easily.

2 **PASTING BRUSH:** Apply paste with a large pasting brush or wall brush with soft, long bristles. Alternatively, use a short-pile paint roller and put the paste in the tray.

3 **PAPERHANGER'S SCISSORS:** These have extra-long blades for straight cuts but any large pair of sharp scissors will do.

PAPERHANGER'S BRUSH: Like a wide paintbrush with a stumpy handle, this is for smoothing the paper onto the wall. The bristles must be soft enough not to damage the paper, but stiff enough to be poked into corners and force out excess paste.

SEAM ROLLER: A small wood or plastic roller that can be run up and down the seams to press down the paper so that it won't lift when dry. Rubber smoothing rollers squeeze trapped air from under the paper. Use a felt roller for delicate papers. Don't use a seam roller on textured paper.

RETRACTABLE TAPE MEASURE, PLUMB LINE AND SPIRIT LEVEL: Essential for helping you to mark the position of the paper.

Handywoman helpline

Q: How on earth do I work out how much wallpaper I'll need for the job?

A: Wallpaper comes in standard widths and lengths – approximately 1050cm (34 feet) long and 530mm (21 inches) wide. To calculate what you need, measure the wall height from ceiling to skirting board and add 100mm (4 inches) for trimming to get the length. Work out how many lengths you can get from one roll of wallpaper – four strips is average. Measure round the perimeter of the room (ignoring windows and doors) to find out how many roll widths you will need. Divide this by the number of lengths you can cut from one length to give the number of rolls required.

Add to this an allowance for matching any pattern (the length of the repeat will be given on the label) and add a little more for mistakes and accidents. Look out for handy calculating charts in DIY stores and decorating shops.

Wallpaper prep

Prepare walls as for painting but seal newly plastered walls with a proprietary size or diluted wallpaper paste so that the wallpaper will stick.

Order of work

Finish painting ceilings and woodwork before applying wallpaper.

Papering around a door

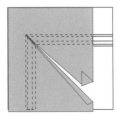

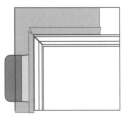

Allow a length of wallpaper to fall across the door then make a diagonal cut towards the corner of the doorframe. Brush the paper into place along the side of the frame, then score with scissors around the frame and trim, leaving 12mm (½ inch) along the top edge for the piece above the frame. Brush down the remaining paper above the door and trim along the top of the frame.

Papering around a window

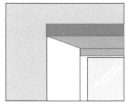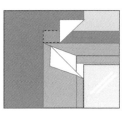

For a neat edge around a window reveal, paper the top of the reveal first, then paper over the overlap and cut along the edge as if you were papering around a door (see opposite).

Papering around a radiator

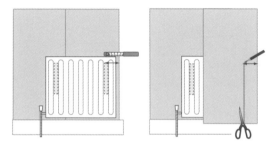

Mark the position of the radiator bracket and cut the paper from the bottom, up the length of the bracket. Push the paper into position around the bracket using a long-handled brush.

Papering around a light switch

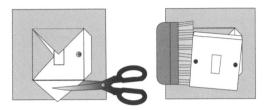

When you come to a light switch or electric socket, allow the paper to fall across the switch (turn off the electricity first), push scissors through the paper at the centre of the switch and make 4 diagonal cuts towards the corners. Tap the paper into place around the edge of the faceplate and trim off the excess, leaving 5 mm (¼ inch) all round. Unscrew the faceplate, tuck the paper behind and screw back into position. Wait until the paste is dry before turning the electricity back on.

Did you know that...?

...thin paper will show up any small imperfections in the underlying surface and will highlight larger ones.

...wobbly walls and less-than-straight edges will be emphasised by stripes or large patterns.

...damp walls are not good for wallpaper unless you can waterproof the surface beforehand with PVA or special sealer.

...unless paper is coated, the surface will rub off in areas of high wear such as halls and staircases. Furniture will also damage the surface if allowed to come into contact with it.

...porous and non-colourfast papers are not suitable for kitchens or bathrooms or anywhere where they may come into contact with moisture.

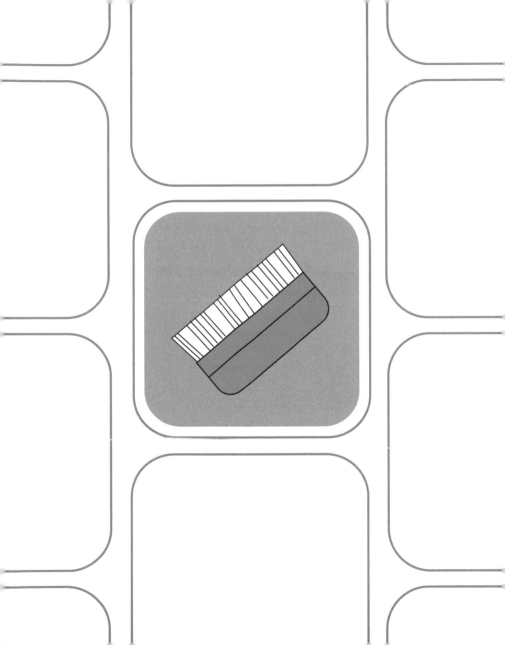

TILING

Seven tiling essentials

1 **TILE CUTTER OR PLATFORM CUTTER:** Used to cut tiles in half. With a tile cutter you have to score the tiles and snap them by hand. A platform cutter is easier and safer to use.

2 **TILE NIBBLERS:** Pincers used to cut narrow strips, small notches and corners from tiles.

3 **TILE SAW:** Used for cutting out curved shapes when fitting tiles round pipes and so forth.

4 **METAL FILE, TILE SANDER AND OILED SLIPSTONE:** Used to smooth down cut edges.

TILE ADHESIVE: Usually sold ready-mixed. Most are water-resistant.

SPACERS: Guides for spacing tiles accurately.

GROUT: Fills the gaps between tiles. Heat-resistant versions for kitchens and epoxy-based versions for germ-free worktops are available.

Handywoman helpline

Q: Yet again, I've got problems working out quantities. How can I calculate how many tiles I need for a job?

A: This isn't too difficult. Measure one of the tiles you'll be using and then work out how many you need for the height and the width of the area to be covered. Multiply the two figures and add 10 per cent (perhaps 15 per cent for beginners) for breakages and mistakes.

Q: And what do I have to do to get the surface ready before I tile?

A: Tiles can be stuck to most surfaces as long as they're flat, clean and dry with no loose paint, plaster or debris. New plaster should be left for several weeks so it dries out properly. Don't tile over wallpaper. Prepare unstable surfaces with a coat of PVA-based adhesive but make sure it's the waterproof variety.

If you've got old tiles, you can remove them, which is messy and laborious, or you can tile on top. Scrape out any loose grout, stick down loose tiles and fill big gaps with filler.

Cutting a margin tile

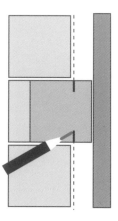

1 Fit margin tiles after all the whole tiles have been put on and mark each one individually as the edges of the wall may not be straight. Place a tile upside down on top of a tile in the last row of whole, fixed tiles and position it against the finished edge. Mark along the edge of the tile, not forgetting to make an allowance for the spacing and for any grouting if necessary.

2 Use the marks to cut the margin tile to size. Spread adhesive on the back and press into position.

Tiling a splashback

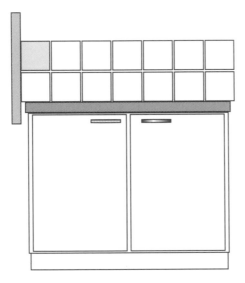

1 Measure and mark out the position of the tiles and, using a batten as a guide, work in rows starting in a top corner.

2 When tiling in a recess or lining the tiles up exactly with the edge of units mark the centre line and work out towards the edges.

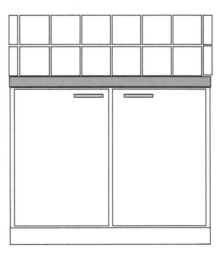

Tiling behind a unit

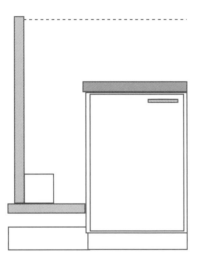

1 For tiled areas that extend beyond and around units, place one batten along the side and another along the line of the bottom of the lowest whole tile. Place the first tile where these battens join.

2 Take away the battens before measuring, cutting and positioning the final margin tiles (see page 142).

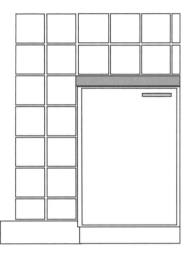

Grouting tiles

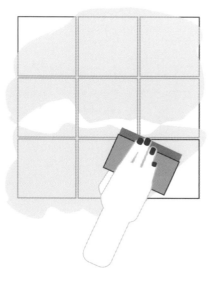

1 Allow 24 hours for the adhesive to harden before grouting. Using a rubber-bladed spreader or dense foam sponge, spread grout in all directions, forcing it into all the gaps. Wipe grout from the surface of the tiles using a barely damp sponge.

2 When the grout has dried, polish the tiles with a dry cloth.

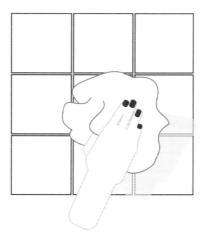

Applying mosaic tiles

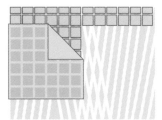

1 Mosaic tiles are normally supplied in sheets on a mesh backing or with a facing paper that is removed after application.

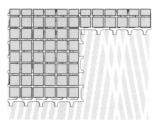

2 Keep the spaces between the sheets of mosaic the same as the space between individual tiles and fill in the margins by cutting strips or single tiles from the sheet using tile nibblers to cut to size.

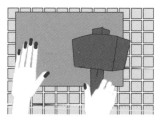

3 In order to make sure the tiles are bedded properly, apply pressure with a piece of board covered in a soft material such as carpet, and tap gently with a wooden mallet.

Tiling around a socket

When you tile around an electricity socket or a light switch you need to leave a space for the wiring. You also need to make absolutely sure that you're working safely and that means turning off the power before you start and not re-connecting it until everything has dried out. Follow these 3 simple steps for socket success.

1 Switch off the electricity, unscrew the socket and pull it away from the wall. Loosely fit the tile or tiles on the wall where the socket will be. Push the socket back as far as you can and mark the position of the socket on the tiles in pencil.

2 Remove the tiles from the wall and cut them inside the pencil line so that when the socket is back in place, there is room for the wires but the socket will sit on top of the tiles.

3 Fix the tiles and grout. When the tile adhesive and grouting are completely dry, screw the socket back in place and turn the power back on.

FLOORS,
WALLS &
CEILINGS

Bare is beautiful

... especially if it's limestone, old waxed boards, polished concrete or brand new solid wood. Ordinary floorboards can look good when sanded, painted, varnished or waxed. Old tiles, flagstones and even concrete can look beautiful if cleaned up and sealed.

but...

...hard floors can be cold, especially in winter – even with the best central heating.

...the ventilation under a wooden floor can be a draught if floorboard gaps are too wide.

...bare floors are noisy, particularly when made of hard materials such as tiles that don't absorb any sound.

...before laying an impervious floor covering such as laminate or vinyl, make sure that it won't prevent air circulating below the floor as this can lead to dry rot.

Carpet pros and cons

✳ It's often cheaper and easier to carpet a room than fiddle with restoring old floorboards.

✳ Carpet is heavy and difficult to handle. Fitting it round features and getting it neatly into corners isn't easy. A badly fitted carpet will never look good, so maybe it's best to have the job done professionally.

✳ If finances are tight and you're desperate to cheer up a small room cheaply, then do have a go at carpeting it yourself. Avoid expensive thick carpet and opt for thinner foam-backed carpet instead, then if it doesn't look perfect, you haven't wasted a fortune.

✳ Carpet is cosy to walk on.

✳ Carpet can cause allergies.

✳ Stains can be difficult to remove from carpet.

✳ Carpet helps with soundproofing.

Match set

If you want to replace a damaged floorboard,
you have to match it to the others. Cheap
softwood boards, laid as a base rather than a
feature, are usually thin and come in a standard
width that's available from timber yards and
DIY stores. Old floorboards are often wider and
thicker so you may have to go to an architectural
salvage yard to find a replacement – and it
may need a little cleaning up before use.

Replacing a floorboard

Lifting a floorboard should be done with care to avoid damaging the boards next to it.

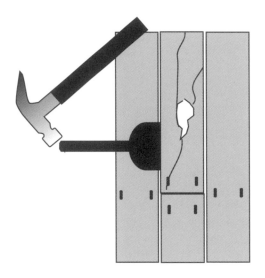

1 Tap the bolster chisel into the gap near to the end of the board to be removed. Lever gently until the board begins to lift and the nails start to come out.

2 Repeat this process at the other end. Insert the claw of a hammer under the lifted board to make room to insert a cold chisel.

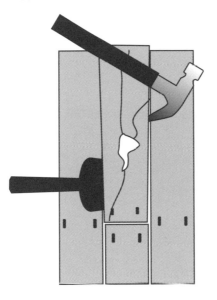

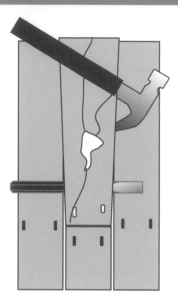

3 Slide the cold chisel underneath the floorboard towards the next set of nails. Repeat this process along the length of the board until it eases out.

4 Fit the new board into position and nail it down to the joist using floorboard nails. Nail at the ends and wherever it crosses a joist.

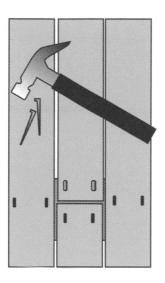

Five typical floor repair problems

If any of the following floorboard problems apply, you may want to seek help from a carpenter:

1 **PROBLEM:** The floorboard you want to replace disappears under the skirting: you'll have to lift it up in order to pull it out. If it's a long board that extends under two skirting boards, then you'll have to cut it in half.

2 **PROBLEM:** The floorboard you want to replace is nailed underneath the skirting: you'll have to cut it as close to the skirting board as possible using a floorboard saw.

3 **PROBLEM:** The floorboards are tongued and grooved: there's no gap for easy levering.

4 **PROBLEM:** The new floorboard sits below the rest of the floor: you will have to put packing underneath (some cardboard, hardboard or thin wood will do) where it is nailed to the joists.

5 **PROBLEM:** The new floorboard stands above the rest of the floor: you'll either have to make the board thinner by planing it or you must cut a recess into the joists to slot the board into.

Sand advice

✻ Sanding creates a lot of dust and noise, so warn your neighbours before you start work.

✻ Boards to be sanded must be sound, not too uneven and not full of holes.

✻ If you already have polished floorboards in good condition but feel they're a bit dull or dark, think hard before doing any sanding. Simply cleaning and re-waxing will lighten them and restore them to a glory you didn't know they had.

✻ Solid wood parquet floors should be left to the experts; don't risk spoiling them with home sanding.

✻ Before you start sanding, fix any loose floorboards and knock any protruding nail heads below the surface. Remove all furnishings, curtains and so forth and open all the

windows. Seal gaps around the door with tape and wedge newspaper at the bottom. Hang a wet sheet on the outside of the door to help prevent the dust escaping.

✳ The sanding machine won't necessarily behave as you would expect it to. It will try to run away, so don't let go.

✳ Hold the drum off the floor when you switch it on and lower it gently to begin sanding. Once switched on, keep moving: leaving the sander in one spot for any length of time will result in a hollow in the floor.

✳ Wear a mask, goggles and ear protection.

Sanding a wooden floor

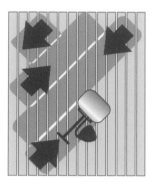

1 Using a coarse abrasive paper, sand the floor diagonally, tilting the machine to change direction and overlapping each run to ensure the whole surface is sanded. When you've done the whole floor, switch off, sweep up the dust and start again, this time sanding diagonally in the opposite direction.

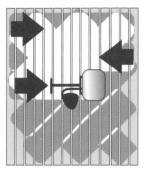

2 Once the floor is flat, change to a medium-grade paper and sand across the boards.

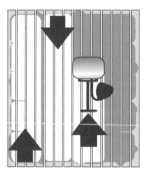

3 Using a fine-grade paper, sand up and down until the surface is smooth and scratch-free.

The perfect finish

Sealants for wooden floors divide roughly into varnishes and oils. Varnish can be applied by brush directly onto new or newly finished wood and will need two or more coats to form a hard, durable surface. Choose between a shiny or a matt finish. Sanding by hand between coats will give a better result.

Finishing oils soak into wood and plump up the fibres. Modern versions have additives to help form a waterproof and dirt-proof surface. Waxing on top of these will produce a soft, mellow finish that will mature well.

For less-than-perfect wood, a darker finish will disguise a multitude of sins. Avoid using wood stains as it can be difficult to achieve an even finish. Instead use a coloured wood varnish. Most of these are available in different wood colours. Using a dark colour will give a similar effect to a wood stain but with less hassle.

Stone

Stone or slate flags are full of character and add a sense of history, but they can also look stunning in a pared-down, modern interior. Damaged or pitted surfaces are part of their character. To restore, scrape off any old dirt or paint and scrub with soap and water or with a specialist stone cleaner. Fill any gaps using cement-based exterior filler, then finish with the appropriate sealer, which will soak into the stone and prevent dirt penetrating.

Tile

Tiled floors are often found in older properties. If their condition isn't great they may respond to a good clean, re-grout and seal. You could freshen up a modern ceramic tiled floor by re-grouting with a new colour.

Concrete

If you have an old concrete floor and are keen on the brutal, industrial look, you can patch it up and paint it or simply seal it. Clean out holes and cracks, removing any loose material, then get rid of all the dust with a vacuum cleaner. Fill any gaps using cement-based exterior filler. Concrete is dusty, so you'll have to seal it if it's to be left uncovered.

Laying laminate

Laminated flooring comes in a range of lengths, widths, materials and prices. Planks or sections fit together with a tongue-and-groove joint for a seam-free surface. New systems don't require adhesive.

They can be laid on top of boards, concrete or any level surface and are usually bought in kits that include spacers and a tamping block (for tapping joints together).

1 Cover the entire floor with underlay, joining the strips together using adhesive tape. If the sub-floor is made of concrete, lay down a thick sheet of plastic to prevent moisture rising up through the underlay.

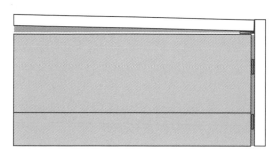

2 Place the grooved side of a laminate strip along the longest wall. Put spacers in between to create an expansion gap. Insert the grooved side of a second strip into the first. Repeat until you are close to the wall. Cut the last strip to fit, allowing for an expansion gap.

3 Cut lengths of quadrant beading to fit around the room to cover the expansion gap. Use a mitre block to cut the angled joints for the corners (see page 69). Nail the quadrant beading in place with panel pins.

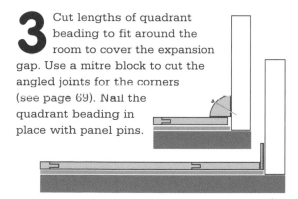

Handywoman helpline

Q: A wall's just a wall isn't it? Why do I need to know if it's anything special?

A: There are lots of different types and you need to know what you've got. First come solid walls – stone, brick, concrete block or solid concrete. Inside walls are normally covered with plaster but if they're old stone, they will be coarsely rendered.

Old properties may have inside walls of lath – strips of wood nailed to a framework and covered with lime-based plaster. Depending on the building's condition, this can be hard and strong or weak and crumbly.

A cavity wall is a double external wall with a gap in between which may be filled with insulation material.

A stud partition wall is a wooden framework with plaster-board nailed to it. This is often skimmed with a thin layer of plaster to give a smooth finish.

Then there are structural walls and non-structural walls. Structural walls support a building. If you want to remove one you need to replace it, usually with an RSJ (rolled steel joist). Definitely one for the builder!

Non-structural walls do what it says on the tin, so you can take them away without the building falling down. Only an expert will know which are non-structural walls so DON'T do it yourself.

Warning signs

Very uneven, undulating surfaces on walls and ceilings are part of the character of an old property but in newer buildings it could be a sign of something wrong, so get them looked at.

Fine cracks in plaster are often the result of shrinkage due to drying, heat, and so on, or vibration from impact such as knocking in nails or drilling a hole. Bigger cracks appear through settlement due to minor building work in adjacent rooms or properties, or are the result of unusually extreme temperatures. Large cracks or cracks that keep getting bigger can indicate structural faults, so get a professional to have a look.

Ceiling special

✳ If you're a novice don't drill into a ceiling. There will certainly be electric wires and maybe heating and water pipes, plus ceilings aren't usually solid, which makes the whole procedure a risky business.

✳ Ceilings usually consist of plasterboard nailed to wooden joists. The plasterboard is then plastered. In older houses the plaster is applied to lath (see page 179) and the plaster may be thick enough for a fairly deep hole. If you want to attach something to a newer, thinner plasterboard ceiling, use a threaded fixing.

✳ If you want to hang something heavy from the ceiling you have to find a joist to give you something solid to screw into. Tap along the ceiling until you find an area that doesn't sound hollow. If this extends right across the ceiling then you've probably found a joist.

The whole truth

✳ Working on holes in ceilings gives you a pain in the neck.

✳ Small to medium-sized cracks, holes and dents in walls and ceilings can be filled using an all-purpose filler. Apply using a filling knife or flat scraper and leave the filler slightly proud of the surface since it will shrink slightly when it dries. Once dry, use sandpaper to smooth out the bumps.

✳ For bigger, deeper holes use bonding – a lightweight coarse plaster mix. When it's dry, rub down with coarse sandpaper before applying a top layer of smooth filler.

✳ Seriously big holes normally involve a bit of re-plastering. If you value your property and your sanity, call in an expert plasterer.

✳ Getting filler into the gaps around door- and window frames, skirting boards and the joins between walls and ceilings, can be fiddly and messy, so use a ready-mixed flexible acrylic filler that fits into an applicator gun.

Shortcut to hole-filling success

Old screw holes are often quite deep so poke some bits of damp newspaper into the hole before applying the filler.

WINDOWS
& DOORS

Squeaky doors

Squeaky doors may add atmosphere in a horror film but they're irritating. A squirt of oil on the hinges will solve the problem. If this doesn't work, or only works for a short while, it may be that the door isn't hanging properly (see page 189).

Rattling doors

If the door rattles and doesn't close properly it could be that the latch doesn't fit into the latch keep. If this is the case, take off the keep and pack it out with some card or wood filler, remembering that you may need slightly longer screws when you put it back.

Alternatively, the keep may be too near and the latch doesn't have room to spring into the cavity, in which case remove the keep and chisel out a little more wood from the recess before screwing it back into place.

Handywoman helpline

Q: My door doesn't seem to fit properly. Do I have to take the door off to make it fit better?

A: Not necessarily. Look at the hinges and check that the screws are all present and tight, that the hinges fit flush with the frame and that they're positioned so that the door hangs at 90 degrees. Sometimes the screws work loose and tightening them, or replacing them with slightly longer screws, will pull the door back into position.

If the door still won't shut, find the place where it isn't fitting into the frame and either sand it down or plane off the excess (you may have to take the door off to do this). ALWAYS make adjustments to the door, NOT the frame.

A bit unhinged

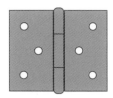

✳ The simplest form of hinge is the butt hinge with two flat rectangular flaps either side of the knuckle. One is screwed to the inside of the doorframe and the other to the edge of the door. They're set into a recess cut to the size and depth of the hinge flap so that they're flush with the woodwork. Just undo the screws on the frame if you need to remove the door.

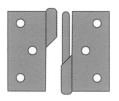

✳ The rising butt hinge lifts the door as it opens to fit over any carpet. The hinge has two sections: one has a spindle and goes on the frame, the other a socket that fits over the spindle. The door can be lifted off without undoing any screws. They come in left- and right-handed opening versions.

Shortcut to hinge success

Worn hinges cause doors to drop and therefore stick. Fitting new hinges of the same size into the existing recess is easy, but use new, slightly larger screws to ensure they fit tightly into the old holes.

Fitting a new door

1 First, find a friend to help hold the door in position. Make sure the door fits into the frame – there should be a gap of 2mm (¹⁄₁₆ inch) at the top and sides and a minimum of 5mm (¼ inch) at the bottom (more if you have thick carpet). To check, stand the door in the frame with wedges underneath to raise the door to the correct height.

2 Make any necessary adjustments to the door edges using a plane. With the door in the correct place, mark the position of the 100mm (4 inch) butt hinges 180mm (7 inches) from the top and 250mm (10 inches) from the bottom on both the door and the frame.

3 Stand the door on its edge with the hinge side uppermost. Place the flap of the opened hinge against the marks, making sure that the knuckle of the hinge projects beyond the edge. Draw round the flap with a pencil and mark the depth along on the edge.

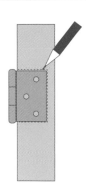

4 Use a chisel to make several cuts (the depth of the hinge) across the marked area, taking care not to cut across the pencil line. Also make cuts around the edge.

5 Pare away the wood to form a recess to fit the hinge flap.

6 Neaten up the finished cut section. Repeat for the other hinge.

7 Put the hinge flap in place and mark and drill pilot holes for the screws.

8 Screw the hinge into place.

9 Wedge the door in an open position with the unscrewed flaps against the marks on the door frame. Making sure the knuckle is parallel to the frame, mark round the flap and repeat the carpentry on the frame.

10 Hang the door first using only one screw in each hinge and check the door opens and closes smoothly. You may need to make the recesses a little deeper, or pack them out with thin card. Fix the other screws.

All sorts of windows

✳ Sash windows go up and down by means of a cord in the side of the frame.

✳ Casement windows are hinged vertically to open like a door.

✳ Pivot windows have a hinge that allows them to rotate.

The guillotine effect

Broken sash cords won't prevent you from opening a sash window but they won't hold the window open either. Replacing them involves taking the window out of the frame so get an experienced DIYer to do it. Watch how it's done, then you'll be able to tackle the next one yourself.

What's it made of?

Most domestic window frames are made from wood but metal isn't uncommon. Many new frames are made from coated aluminium while others combine wood and metal in units whose construction is surprisingly complicated, so don't even think about taking one out or putting in a new one. They're designed to be virtually maintenance-free so shouldn't require much fixing; if they do, it's best to call in a window specialist.

Play it safe

Broken or cracked windows are dangerous and insecure as well as looking unkempt and unloved. Get a glazier to replace any glass. A professional will measure correctly for the replacement, get it cut, take out the broken bits, fit the new piece and take all the broken glass away. Well worth the money.

If you have those new metal window frames with the glass set into the frame, the glass requires special fitting.

An open and shut case

✳ Windows that open and close easily are a joy. If they don't, it's often over-enthusiastic use of paint either inside or out that prevents them. If the paint is thin, you can carefully cut along the join with a sharp-bladed knife and use a scraper to open up the gap. If it's thick and has seeped through all the joins, you'll have to resort to paint stripper or a hot-air paint stripper (see page 107).

✳ If you can't shut the window properly check where it fits against the frame – especially the hinge edge since paint or dirt may be preventing a good seal. Hinges may also stiffen as a result of overpainting. A small amount of paint stripper may help get things moving. A squirt of oil will also loosen up clogged hinges.

Five handywoman draught-proofing tips

1 The easiest and cheapest form of draught excluder is a flexible foam strip with a peel-off backing that is stuck to the door- or window frame. It works well but gets grubby quickly and will need replacing regularly.

2 Many draught excluders for doors take the form of wood, metal, rubber, plastic or bristles attached to a strip (usually aluminium) that's screwed to the doorframe.

3 Threshold excluders are screwed along the bottom of the door either on the inside or outside. These include weather trims (screwed to the outside of the door and angled to shed water) and brush seals (a row of dense stiff bristles attached to a metal or wooden trim and screwed on the inside of the door).

4 Letterboxes can be very draughty. Fitting an internal flap will help. Some include brush seals but these can be quite fierce and sometimes tear your mail – and your nails.

5 Draught-proofing for windows is much the same as for doors and varies according to the window type and construction. If any solution seems too pricey, too fiddly or will spoil the look of a window or door, consider keeping out draughts with heavy curtains or blinds.

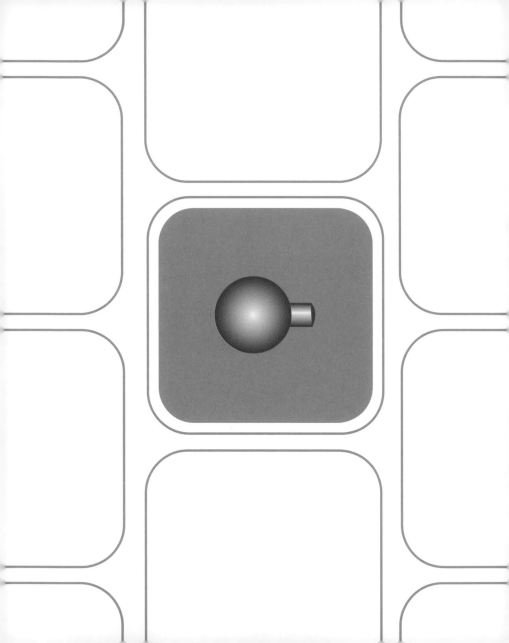

Shortcuts to door furniture success

An otherwise plain door can be transformed into a design feature by the addition of smart new door furniture. Choose from the wide range of traditional or modern designs.

Before buying, make sure you have the correct fitting for your door. The mechanism should either be fitted in a hole in the edge of the door or contained in a casing fitted on the surface of the door, with a latch keep screwed to the edge of the doorframe.

Safe as houses

✳ Some home insurance companies insist on a certain level of security before providing cover. Find out before embarking on any security improvements since certain locks and fittings may be specified.

✳ Once you're inside with all the bolts and locks secured you won't be able to get out easily. Having to fiddle with keys in a fire could be fatal, and if you're taken ill, valuable time could be wasted by people who are trying to get to you.

✳ Make sure keys are kept in an accessible place (but not handy for burglars), leave a spare set with someone reliable and give all details to close friends and family.

Did you know that...?

...window locks are often required for insurance purposes. They work by locking the window to the frame (or in the case of sash windows, locking the windows together) either with a screw or a bolt. They are usually operated with a key. Many use a standard key, which is widely available (and can be bought by burglars) but others have keys that come in several hundred variations.

...newer windows are supplied with integral locks and lockable stays. If you have traditional, wooden windows, it's easy to fix screw-on locks.

...patio doors are especially inviting to intruders, so make sure they're fitted with the correct type of lock and fit them top and bottom to prevent the doors being lifted out of the frame.

Lock, stock and barrel

✳ **LOCKS** are best fitted by a locksmith but if you're simply replacing a lock, it's easy to do providing you get one of similar size and made to fit into the existing holes.

✳ **THE INTERNAL MECHANISM** is all you have to replace – not the entire lock – if your keys have been lost or stolen.

✳ **A CYLINDER RIM LOCK** is used mainly on front doors. A small knob or handle on the inside turns a spring lock to open the door. When the door closes, the spring lock automatically springs back into place and can only be opened from the outside using a key. An extra turn with the key from the outside will (dead)lock it into position so that it can't be opened from the inside.

✳ **A MORTICE LOCK** is fitted into a hole in the edge of the doorframe and must be locked and unlocked with a key, although some can be opened from the inside with a knob or handle.

✷ **HINGE BOLTS** screw into the edge of the door – near the hinges for strength – and fit into a recess in the doorframe when the door is closed.

✷ **RACK BOLTS** fit into the edge of the door and are operated by a key.

✷ **SPYHOLES** are useful for checking out a visitor before choosing whether or not to open the door. They're simple to install and can be adjusted to fit any thickness of door.

✷ **A SECURITY CHAIN** is another wise precaution. The fixed end of the chain is screwed to the door frame and the loose end fits into a fixing plate screwed to the door. For convenience, position it just below the lock.

A welter of window treatments

✳ If you like the pared-down look (and aren't overlooked), leave your windows unadorned. If you value your privacy use etched glass, plastic film or a spray-on frosted-glass-effect paint.

✳ When it comes to curtains, gathers are out. The newest curtains are simple panels, just a tad wider than the window, and they hang straight from ungathered tops.

✳ Cropped curtains are all the rage. No need to have them touching the windowsill or hovering just above the carpet; let them hang out halfway between the window ledge and the floor.

✳ Hang curtains, panels, dhurries or throws from simple poles and attach them with rings, ties, loops, clips or even safety pins.

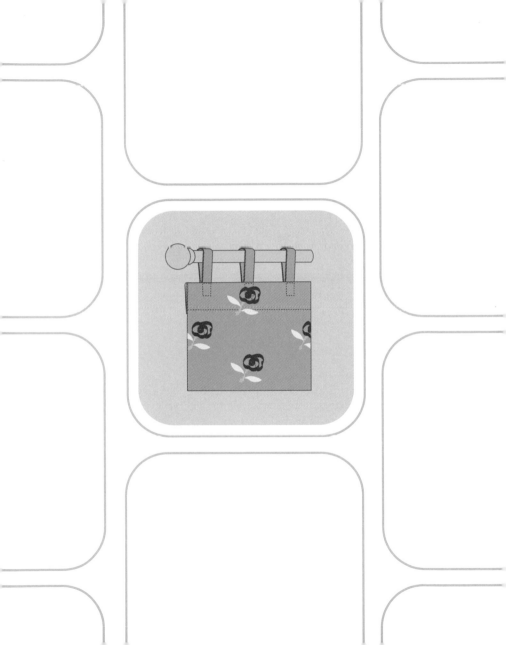

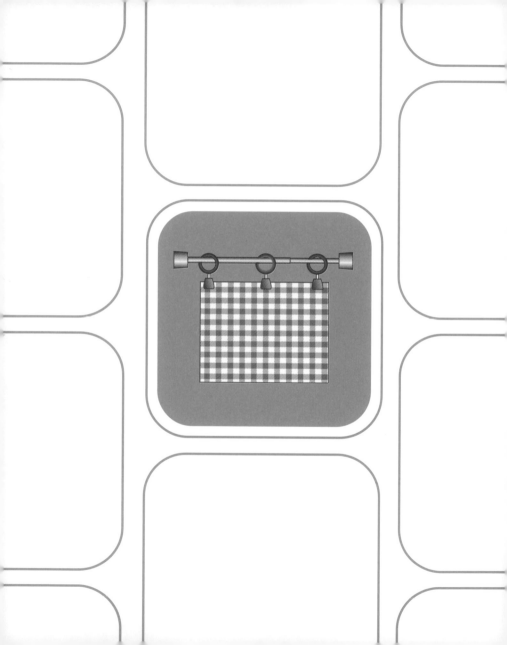

✳ Original old shutters enhance the character of a home. If you don't have them, try perfectly plain ultra-modern shutters or slatted versions instead, which look pleasingly continental or a little colonial.

✳ Make lightweight shutters by stretching fabric onto a frame or threading panels onto poles. Use screw hooks and eyes to fix them.

FURNITURE
& SHELVING

Handywoman helpline

Q: I've got loads of stuff that needs to be stored on shelves but there's so much choice in the shops that my mind goes blank just thinking about it. How can I decide what's best for my purposes?

A: The shelving system you choose will depend on the state of the wall where you want your shelves and what you want to store. Stud partition walls (see page 179) can't support heavy shelves or heavy loads unless you can screw the supports or brackets into the wooden framework. The walls of old properties may be too soft and crumbly to hold screws securely and drilling into stone isn't easy. Some properties have concrete walls that require a very powerful drill for even the smallest job. If drilling into the wall isn't an option, it may be best to choose a freestanding system.

The lowdown on shelving materials

✳ Softwoods such as pine are relatively inexpensive and can be stained and sealed or painted.

✳ Hardwoods such as oak and beech look wonderful but are more expensive and heavier than other shelving materials.

✳ Prem-board is made of strips or blocks of solid wood glued together to form a knot-free surface suitable for sealing or painting.

✳ Plywood is thin layers of wood sandwiched together and glued into sheets. Good for shelves, but should be cut by machine – and the edges will need careful finishing.

✳ Laminated boards are made of chipboard covered with laminate or veneer. Light, convenient and inexpensive.

✳ Stainless steel and wire mesh are great shelving materials but buy them ready-cut and finished as they're difficult to work with.

✳ If you're using glass, always buy the toughened sort and get it cut and finished by a glass supplier.

No visible means of support

The floating shelf, one of the most popular of the 'ready-to-hang' types of shelf, is a box-like construction with a batten-and-bolt system that's entirely concealed within the construction so that the shelf looks as if it's 'floating'. It looks very smart and can be surprisingly inexpensive. Putting one up involves screwing the batten to the wall and securing the shelf to the batten from underneath.

Go it alone

There are a variety of freestanding shelving systems around from very inexpensive wooden or metal units for garage or utility room storage to smarter combinations using high-quality materials. They're ideal if your walls aren't suitable for fixing into, or if you don't want or aren't allowed to drill into them. Easy to take down and re-assemble in a different position according to need or whim, and they can also be used as room dividers.

A brace of brackets

✴ Pressed-steel shelf brackets are cheap and cheerful and can look very chic in an 'industrial' sort of way.

✴ Look out for smarter designs in stainless steel and curved plywood.

✴ Use large, chunky brackets and a slab of wood as a feature shelf.

✴ Use several brackets to support a long shelf. The shelf could even extend around the whole room.

Shortcut to shelving success

Shelving systems using brackets that slot
into metal uprights screwed into the wall
are flexible and involve less drilling.

Four handywoman tips for getting shelving right

1 When fitting shelves inside alcoves take measurements at the back, front and all the way down the alcove as walls are rarely true.

2 Unless you want an exact fit, get all the shelves for an alcove cut to the smallest measurement.

3 To ensure adequate support when putting shelves on brackets, make sure that the bracket spans nearly the whole depth of the shelf and that there's sufficient overhang either side. The amount of overhang will depend on the thickness of the shelf and the weight of the load.

Always use a spirit level for marking and positioning shelves so that they're level. A sloping ceiling and walls may make the shelf look 'out,' but lining up with anything other than the true horizontal and vertical will lead to problems which are structural as well as visual.

Make your own picture shelf

Picture shelves allow you to change the arrangement of favourite artworks without peppering the wall with holes. Large pictures look stunning displayed this way but the shelf needs to be strong and well supported. Make the shelf slightly narrower than the back panel and make lipping that overlaps both edges of the shelf. This provides extra structural strength as well as a ledge against which the pictures can rest.

1 Cut three pieces of wood – a back panel, a shelf and front lipping. For a shelf strong enough to hold pictures in frames, use a back panel that's no less than 19mm (¾ inch) thick and 100–125mm (4–5 inches) wide.

2 Drill pilot holes in the back panel ready for screws to fix it to the wall, then screw and glue it to the shelf for strength.

3 Place the lipping along the front of the shelf, then pin and glue into place.

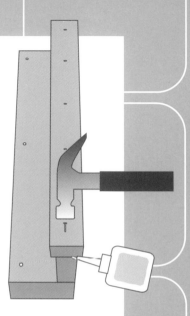

4 Fill over the pin heads, smooth the surfaces and edges with abrasive paper and paint or stain before fixing in place on the wall.

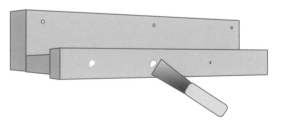

Five steps to fitting a shelf on brackets

1 Mark the position of the shelf on the wall then work out the position of the brackets, allowing for the overhang. If you're using more than two brackets, space them evenly along the length of the shelf, measuring from the centre for accuracy.

2 Hold one bracket to the wall using a spirit level to ensure it's straight and mark the positions of the holes.

3 Drill the holes and screw the bracket to the wall.

4 Hold the next bracket against the wall on its marked position.

5 Place the shelf across both brackets, put a spirit level on top and adjust the position of the second bracket until the shelf is level. Mark the position of the holes and fix as before. If you're using more than two brackets, fix the end ones first.

Off-the-shelf shelves

A variety of 'ready-to-hang' shelves are now available. Some incorporate extras such as hanging rails, plate racks and so forth, while others are plain but are made from materials such as wire mesh, stainless steel or plastic – materials that a DIYer would have difficulty working with. Most can be fixed directly to the wall with screws, so require nothing more than a drill and a spirit level to put them up.

'Off-the-shelf shelves require nothing more than a drill and a spirit level to put them up.'

Be flexible

The simplest flexible shelving systems consist of narrow metal uprights with slots or a single groove along their whole length into which purpose-made metal brackets are fitted.

1 To work out where the uprights need to be positioned, fix the first upright to the wall with the top screw only. Using a spirit level to ensure it's vertical, mark the positions of the other screws.

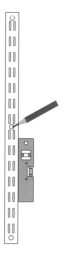

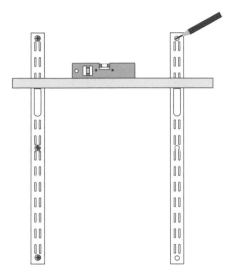

2 Drill at the marked points and screw the first upright to the wall. Insert a bracket near the top of the fixed upright and another in the corresponding position on a second upright. Hold this upright roughly where it's to be fixed to the wall. Place a shelf across the two brackets and, using a spirit level to check, move the upright into the correct position. Mark the top hole, then drill and fix as before.

Shelves on battens

Where shelves span two walls, they can be supported on battens screwed to the walls.

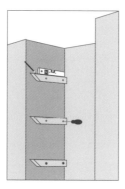

1 Cut the battens to the required length, sand the edges and chamfer (cut at an angle) the ends.

2 Drill pilot holes right through the battens, using a countersink bit to hide the screws. Work out the position of each shelf and mark the position of the battens on one wall only, using a spirit level to check they're horizontal.

3 Starting at the top, fix the first batten to the wall, then place the shelf in position on the fixed batten and on a second batten held in place on the opposite wall. When you are satisfied the shelf is level, mark the position of the second batten with a pencil line or with a bradawl poked through pre-drilled pilot holes.

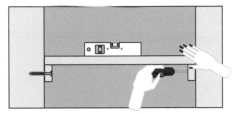

Metal battens

Extruded aluminium battening is an alternative to wood. The batten will normally be cut the full depth of the shelf and will therefore be visible at the front, giving a neat, 'modern' feel. The fitting and suitability for heavy loads will vary according to the design and make.

Make your own fascia shelving

For a neat look, fix a fascia along the front of your shelves. Measure the alcove depth accurately, then cut the battens and shelves short of the outside edge so that when the fascia is added it's flush with the wall.

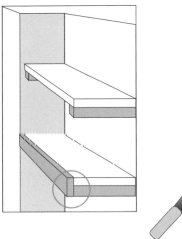

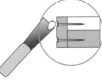

Attach the fascia with long panel pins, tapping them well in so they can be concealed by filler before sealing or painting.

Don't be floored by flatpack

TAKE YOUR TIME: This is the first rule. It always takes longer than you think.

MAKE IT FUN: Plan a day around it: get in plenty of snacks, but avoid alcohol – save that for the celebration or, in extreme circumstances, to forget any disasters afterwards. Don't attempt it if you are feeling grumpy, and don't invite lots of people to help. You just need one other to person as two sets of arms and hands can be useful.

ROOM FOR MANOEUVRE: Allow plenty of space and if the piece of furniture is very large, make sure you will be able to get it into the room it is destined for.

THE RIGHT TOOLS: Make sure you have what you need. Some tools will be included with the kit but you may need screwdrivers, spanners and maybe clamps.

Take Your Time. This is the first rule. It always takes longer than you think.

WHAT'S INSIDE?: Unpack carefully. Examine all the pieces for damage and if any are damaged, pack it all up again and take it back. If you are lucky there will be a list of components and a sheet of instructions. Make sure the pieces look like those in the diagram and that you understand what each is and what it is for.

STILL COUNTING: Count the screws, bolts and fixings and make sure they correspond with what you should have. Sometimes extra screws are included – make sure you are aware of this to avoid the panic induced by the sight of two large screws glinting ominously alongside what's an apparently fully assembled piece of furniture.

BOXING CLEVER: Avoid tearing the cardboard box, keep it, open it out and use it to work on. It will protect the parts – and the floor – from accidental scratches.

Make your own daybed on castors

A good-looking, strong daybed is simple to make using robust castors screwed to a solid-core fire door. This is strong enough to withstand a heavy weight and thick enough to hold the castors securely. Choose swivel-type castors that have reasonably large wheels and preferably rubber tyres.

1 Use six castors for strength, mark their position accurately and don't put them too near the edges.

2 Screw the castors into position, check they move freely and that the base is level. If the castor fixing is deeper than the base, screw blocks of wood to the base first.

SERVICES

Don't DIY

The installation and maintenance of fittings and appliances such as hot-water systems and central-heating boilers are subject to strict regulations. Any major work should always be carried out by a registered installer – failure to do this could affect any insurance claim should an accident occur. Never touch anything involving your gas supply connection; the consequences of getting it wrong can be catastrophic. Always employ a registered professional.

Direct or indirect?

Most homes are connected to a mains water supply that enters the property through the household stopcock (see page 255). Water is then distributed via a system of pipes to feed central-heating systems, tanks, cisterns, taps and appliances such as washing machines and dishwashers.

If you have a direct system, the water for all boilers, cisterns and taps is drawn directly from the mains. With an indirect, stored-water system, only some of the taps are connected directly to the mains. The remaining ones are fed from a cold-water storage tank (usually in the roof space) that supplies the hot-water tank, boiler, cisterns, baths, showers and basins.

Handywoman helpline

Q: Why have I got good water pressure down in my kitchen, but the water comes out in a trickle in the upstairs basins and shower?

A: Water pressure is normally strong in parts of the system that are near to the mains but can be less powerful on upper storeys, especially if the position of the water-storage tank means there's an insufficient head of water to provide a good flow. If lack of pressure is a problem, ask the advice of a good plumber who may suggest new pipework, the re-siting of water tanks or the installation of a pump.

Where does it all go?

All waste is channelled to the mains drainage system. Baths, showers, basins and washing machines eventually drain into a single pipe connected to the mains drainage, but the toilet is connected to a separate soil pipe. These two systems join up with the rainwater collection pipe and then all three are channelled via an inspection chamber (often referred to as a manhole) to the mains drain.

Is your house trying to tell you something?

Minor incidents such as a dripping tap or a blown fuse are irritating but not life-threatening and can be easily remedied. However, they can also be an indication of something wrong with the water or electrical system or a worse problem elsewhere. If you often have to replace fuses or lightbulbs, it could be due to a fault in the wiring and if the sound of a dripping tap doesn't drive you mad, the realisation that the drips have seeped through somewhere and formed an extremely large puddle can make you very cross indeed.

Need to know basis

You need to know where your stop valve or stopcock is located. This is your first port of call if you have a leak as it enables you to turn off the water supply straight away. Mostly the valve is found where the supply enters your home, but it could be outside or even under the floor. You may have stopcocks for specific parts of the system, such as the bathroom or the central-heating system.

Problems with your waterworks

✴ In case of a sudden and dramatic leak, turn off the stopcock straight away. If the source of the leak isn't immediately apparent, call a plumber out.

✴ Hairline cracks in pipes are difficult to detect and as the leaked water often travels along the outside of the pipe before dripping off, the location of the wet patch doesn't always coincide with the leak. If possible, repair the pipe temporarily by binding it with amalgam tape, then call in a plumber.

✴ Water can get through extremely small gaps such as the mastic seals around baths, sinks and basins. Remove all traces of old mastic using a special solvent and replace, making sure that all surfaces are perfectly dry when applying.

✳ Areas behind bath panels, sinks, washing machines and dishwashers are particularly vulnerable to leaks so take a look from time to time. Common causes are loose fittings, worn threads and worn washers. Try tightening everything up using a spanner if necessary (but don't force).

HANDYWOMAN BATHTIME TIP
When sealing around a bath, fill it with water and leave until the mastic has set. If you don't, the combined weight of water and bather will pull the mastic away from the wall and break the seal.

Drip, drip!

The most common reason for a tap to drip is a worn washer. If you have traditional taps then changing a washer isn't complicated.

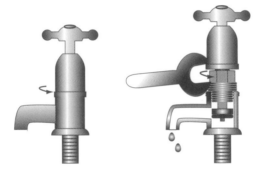

1 Turn off the water at the stop valve. Unscrew the cover and lift to reveal the head-gear nut, then unscrew this using a spanner.

2 Lift out the top section of the tap, remove the old washer and replace with a new one of the correct size.

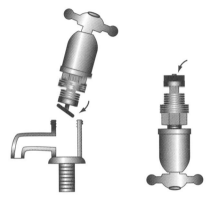

Four ways to clear a blockage

1 Sinks and basins are normally fitted with a plastic trap with an access cap, which can be unscrewed to allow blockages to be cleared.

2 There may also be an access cap on the branch pipe that can be cleared using a wire coat hanger.

3 Caustic soda is a highly efficient shifter of blockages but should be used with care. Follow the instructions on the packet.

4 If the problem persists, it may indicate a more serious blockage further down the pipework. If you're unsure, call in that plumber!

To fill or not to fill?

✳ If your toilet cistern isn't filling, remove the lid and check that the floating valve (also known as a ballcock) is securely attached to the float arm.

✳ If the cistern is filling continuously, you should check that the valve is working. If water is constantly running into the cistern, you may need a new siphon.

✳ If water is pouring out through the overflow, check that the float is adjusted so that the level of water is below the overflow outlet.

Did you know that...?

...electricity is conducted along cables and flexes through, usually, copper wire. The earth beneath our feet is also a very efficient conductor of electricity and any that escapes through exposed or unconnected wires will flow towards the ground, taking the shortest route and passing through any object in its way. If you happen to be touching that object, or are the object itself, the consequences can range from a mild shock to instant death.

That's why an earth wire to channel wayward electric current is included in wiring systems. An earth fault won't necessarily cause the circuit to cut out, but earth-leakage protection will break the circuit when any leakage passes through an outside conductor.

Earth-leakage protection can be included in the consumer unit so the home's entire electricity supply is protected. Otherwise it can be provided for individual appliances by using an earth-leakage protection socket, that plugs into the wall socket.

Blow-out!

Each electrical circuit in the home is connected to a circuit breaker. This has a fuse that blows if there's an electrical fault. Most modern circuit breakers are in the form of a switch that's thrown when the fuse blows. When the problem has been identified and dealt with, the switch can be switched back to the 'on' position.

Water and electricity don't mix

Water is a very good conductor of electricity and great care should be taken not to mix the two. There are rules governing the positioning of electrical outlets in bathrooms and kitchens – which is why you have pull-cord switches in a bathroom and no sockets or switches near sinks.

✳ Always get a qualified electrician to carry out any work in kitchens and bathrooms.

✳ Don't operate switches with wet hands and keep all appliances a safe distance from the water source.

✳ Never use an extension cable in a bathroom to plug in appliances such as heaters.

✳ Warning! Don't switch circuits back on or replace fuses until the problem has been identified and dealt with. If in doubt, consult an electrician.

Handywoman helpline

Q: I never seem to have enough sockets for all the appliances that I need to plug in. Are there any solutions apart from having to get extra sockets put in?

A: The number of appliances we use has increased enormously in recent years and few homes have enough sockets. To avoid dangerously overloaded sockets, use a trailing socket plugged into a single 13-amp wall socket. A trailing socket can provide between two and six 13-amp socket outlets.

Trailing sockets are ideal for items such as computers, printers and lamps, which are relatively low wattage. Such sockets, however, shouldn't be abused: it's better to get an electrician to put in extra sockets than risk overloading the circuit.

Don't blow your fuse

Make sure the fuse in the plug is the correct rating for the appliance. Don't use a high-amp fuse in a low-amp appliance: if a fault occurs the fuse won't blow and that could be dangerous.

✳ Plugs on computer equipment, stereo systems, radios and lamps are normally fitted with a 5-amp fuse.

✳ Kettles, irons and hairdryers require a lot of power to produce heat so plugs should be fitted with a 13-amp fuse.

✳ Cookers should always be connected to their own dedicated circuit with a socket and a 30-amp fuse.

✳ Washing machines and refrigerators can be plugged into a normal socket with a 13-amp fuse.

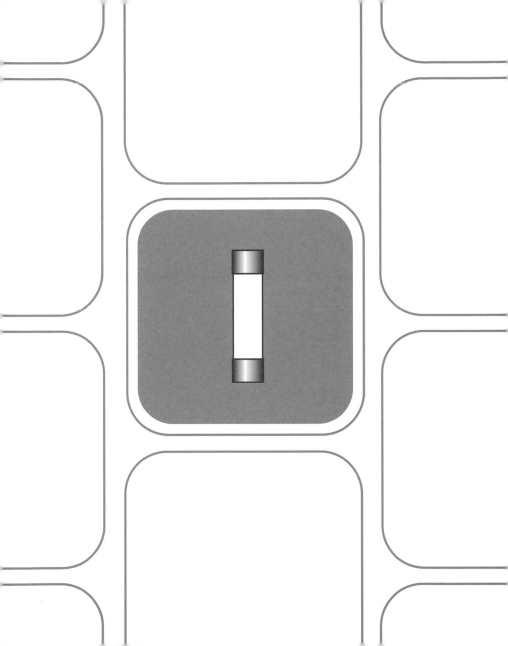

Did you know that...?

...many lighting systems are now low-voltage, operating at 12 or 24 volts. They need a transformer to reduce the mains voltage. When buying a reputable brand, the transformer is normally included, either incorporated in the light fitting itself, in the plug, in a separate plug-in section on the flex, or sometimes in the lightbulb. If you need a separate transformer, specifications and instructions on connection will be included.

Computer control

Unless computer and entertainment equipment cables and flexes are kept under control they can look unsightly. Hide them away altogether, feed them through specially designed cable covers or turn them into a feature.

✳ Keep cables organised, labelled if necessary, and accessible.

✳ Keep all wiring safe from accidental disconnection by feet, children and pets. The simplest way is to gather the wires together and tie them with plastic wire ties, string or even fancy ribbon. Screw cup hooks under a desk or table and loop them up out of sight and out of danger.

✳ Use flexible plastic sleeving through which several cables can be fed for a neat, businesslike look. Alternatively, fix panels to walls, table backs or desk legs to hide all cables and plugs.

✳ Place TVs and sound systems on lidded boxes or chests. Drill holes so any cables can be fed through and kept inside. Drill holes in shelves or use bracketed shelving systems with gaps at the back.

Power surge

Power surges often occur in our electricity supply, sometimes from faults on our own circuits but also occasionally in the supply from the electricity provider. Computers and other electronic equipment can be sensitive to such surges so it's a good idea to use plugs or trailing sockets fitted with a surge suppressor. Alternatively, get an electrician to fit a special socket.

CLEANING

Ten cleaning basics

1

BROOM: For sweeping up. Soft bristles will gather the dust as well as the bits, and will poke more easily into corners.

2

DUSTPAN AND BRUSH: Essential not only for the collection and disposal of sweepings but also a safe way to gather up broken glass or china and nasties such as pet poo or the odd dead mouse.

3

MOP: You can get down on your hands and knees to clean a floor but using a mop is easier. You'll need a wet mop for washing and a dry one for dusting floors.

4 **BUCKET:** Everyone needs a bucket. Plastic is cheap and cheerful, but chic. Galvanised metal, stainless steel and white enamel are very designer but also heavy and noisy.

5 **CLOTHS AND DUSTERS:** Whether you invest in the latest hi-tech duster or just use an old vest, a plentiful selection of cleaning cloths is essential. Use cotton dishcloths, fluffy dusters and linen scrim.

 SCRUBBING BRUSHES: Sometimes a good old-fashioned scrub is the only way to get things clean. Choose from bristles and wood or trendy modern plastic.

7 **SCOURERS:** Flat, nylon scourers are good for cleaning pans but are also great for scrubbing off built-up dirt and deposits, for example on wood-work in preparation for a re-paint.

8 **TOOTHBRUSHES:** There are 101 uses for an old toothbrush. Cleaning round taps, in the corners of window frames and in the crevices of ornaments are just three.

 VACUUM CLEANER: A vacuum cleaner is the domestic equivalent of a best friend. It's the only really efficient way of removing dust and can be used for everything from floors to furniture.

SPONGES: Available in lots of shapes, sizes and compositions. Big foam ones are fine for sloshing on lots of suds but not so good at mopping them up. Heavier ones are more absorbent, while small, natural sponges are great for cleaning delicate objects.

Handywoman helpline

Q: I'm bewildered by the range of cleaning products on the market. What do I really need to do the job?

A: Cream cleansers are slightly abrasive but won't damage smooth surfaces. Use on sinks, baths, loos and very grubby or stained worktops.

✸ General-purpose floor and wall cleaners are for mopping floors and washing worktops, kitchen surfaces and paintwork. They're non-abrasive and so are ideal for wiping down cookers and appliances as they dissolve grease as well as dirt.

✸ Window and glass cleaners do what they say. Several contain vinegar, which adds to their cleaning power.

✸ Chlorine bleach kills germs and bleaches. Use for plugholes, sinks and loos and for sterilising worktops, equipment and so forth. Use a weak solution for washing down or soaking and a stronger solution, or neat, for bleaching out stains.

✸ Mild soap and detergent are suitable for cleaning delicate surfaces and as a frequent-wash cleaner. Old-fashioned blocks of household soap are mild and relatively free from added chemicals. Eco-friendly brands are also available.

Eight handywoman floor-cleaning tips

1 A vacuum cleaner is the most effective way of removing dust and can be used on all floors (but don't use the beating type of vacuum cleaner on hard or shiny floors as they'll get scratched).

2 Use vacuum cleaner tools to suck up dust around edges and underneath things.

3 Keep a broom, dusting mop or carpet sweeper handy for crumbs, spills and things brought in on the soles of shoes.

4 Remove dirt and grease from vinyl, concrete and ceramic floors with a proprietary floor cleaner.

5 For stone floors use soap.

6 To prevent smears on shiny floor tiles, dry with an old towel or absorbent cloth.

7 Non-glazed tiles absorb more dirt and may need an occasional good scrub using a slightly abrasive cleaner. Don't use soap as it will leave a dull film.

8 Clean the grout between floor tiles with detergent or an abrasive cleaner on a brush.

Don't even think about it!

Don't use water on wooden floors, although polyurethane varnish or laminated floor finishes can be mopped or washed using warm water with a few drops of mild detergent and a very well-squeezed-out cloth or mop.

For waxed or oiled floors, vacuum or dust frequently using a dusting mop. Only re-wax if the floor is dull or very dirty.

Handywoman helpline

Q: I've seen several multi-purpose floor-cleaning products that promise protection, stain-resistance and instant shine. Are they worth the money?

A: Use these products with caution as they often build up over time into a coating that becomes dull, dirty and worn. And what's more, they're difficult to remove.

Worktop wizard

✱ Worktops should be washed or wiped down frequently using a clean cloth. A solution of bleach will kill germs.

✱ Wooden worktops need occasional re-oiling, but you can dab sunflower oil on dry patches in between.

✱ Never allow lemon juice to come into contact with stone worktops: it burns into the surface.

Shortcuts to stain-removal success

✳ Tea, coffee, red wine and cola can be removed with soda water. Mop up any excess, pour on soda water and soak up with clean rags. You shouldn't have to rub, but if you do, always work from the outside in to avoid spreading the stain.

✳ Keep a proprietary spot cleaner handy for difficult stains such as ink or dye; apply immediately and then follow the instructions.

✳ Tackle stains in stainless steel or porcelain sinks with cream cleanser or, if that fails, with a solution of chlorine bleach.

Handywoman tips for cleaning...

...**WINDOWS** Use a spray window-cleaner and rub off with clean, lint-free cloths. If very dirty, wash with warm water and detergent first, dry thoroughly, then use the spray.

...**PAINTED WALLS** Remove marks using a mild detergent and a sponge or cloth, though this may remove the paint and leave a discoloured patch. Re-painting is often best.

...**LIMESCALE** Use fizzy limescale-remover tablets in the loo and liquid remover for taps.

...**PLASTIC AND METAL** A duster slightly dampened with a little water or spray cleaner works well.

...**UPHOLSTERY** A vacuum cleaner with a good set of tools works best.

'A vacuum cleaner with a good set of tools works best for upholstery.'

...**WOOD** Give wood an occasional polish with a good-quality wax polish.

...**TAPS** Use cream toothpaste. Rub on with your fingers and rinse well.

...**SLATTED BLINDS** Clean in the shower or bath using the shower attachment, a soft brush and mild detergent.

...**GLASS VASES** Fill with warm water, drop in a couple of denture-cleaning tablets and allow to soak overnight.

...**MILDEW STAINS** Clean off walls with a mild solution of bleach.

...**WALLPAPER** Remove stains and marks by rubbing them gently with white bread.

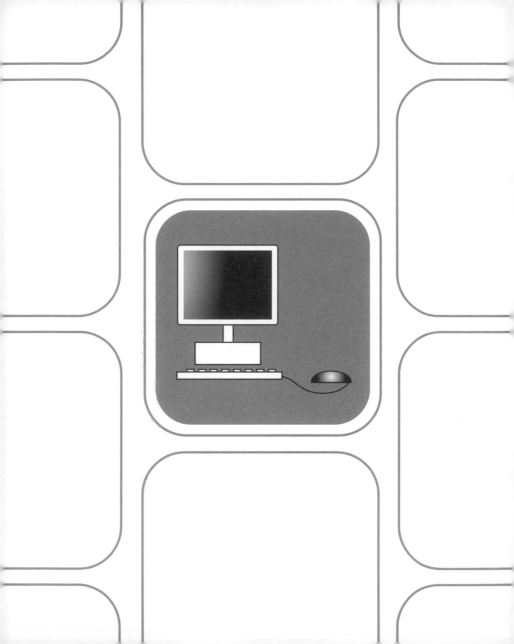

Getting rid of static

Electrical equipment, such as TVs and computers, attract dust via static electricity. Remove frequently with a vacuum cleaner – use the brush attachment on the computer keyboard – or use a duster dampened with an antistatic cleaner.

Computer clean-up

Don't use liquids on computers. Instead invest in computer screen-cleaning wipes.

I haven't got a thing to wear!

When you're cleaning, you really must dress the part. Gloves – rubber for wet work, fleecy-lined for dusting – are essential for protecting those hands and nails. And why not buy yourself a special cleaning outfit – perhaps a huge printed shirt, a fun headscarf and a pair of brightly coloured joggers?

Finally, keep your cleaning materials in a nice box or basket to complement the décor. It will encourage you to use them more often, too.

Handywoman goes eco-friendly

✳ Make your own non-scratch cleanser by mixing ¾ of a cup of baking soda with ¼ cup of borax and enough washing-up liquid to form a smooth paste.

✳ Neat white vinegar is good for removing scum and soap build-up in baths and showers. Use diluted to clean windows and mirrors. Will neutralise odours, including pet accidents. Use with baking soda to make foaming cleansers. As it's acidic, don't use on porous surfaces such as grouting.

✳ Lemon juice is a natural bleach and disinfectant. Use instead of bleach to remove stains on clothes, worktops and hands. Take care and never allow it to come into contact with any form of stone because it burns.

✳ Borax is a general-purpose cleaner that's been around for centuries. Not as corrosive as vinegar or lemon juice.

✳ Baking soda has abrasive and deodorising properties and is brilliant at removing stains. Can be used on clothes, carpets and wallpaper as well as on stained teapots, vacuum flasks and casserole dishes. Dissolves grease and mineral deposits and makes a powerful cleanser for sinks when mixed with vinegar.

✳ Keep moths away with cedar wood and lavender rather than with mothballs.

index